THINKING AHEAD FOR BUSINESS

Thinking Ahead for Business

EDITED BY
EDWARD C. BURSK
EDITOR OF THE *Harvard Business Review* AND
MEMBER OF THE FACULTY, HARVARD GRADUATE
SCHOOL OF BUSINESS ADMINISTRATION

CAMBRIDGE, MASSACHUSETTS
HARVARD UNIVERSITY PRESS
1952

Distributed in Great Britain by
Geoffrey Cumberlege
Oxford University Press
London

Library of Congress Catalog Card Number 52–5388
Printed in the United States of America

PREFACE

This book is based on the proceedings of the Twenty-First National Business Conference, sponsored by the Harvard Business School Association, June 9, 1951. The purpose of the Conference was "to consider the major political, economic and sociological forces throughout the world which promise to have such a profound effect on the future course of American business." The questions posed were: (1) "What are the patterns and prospects of these forces?" and (2) "What problems, opportunities, and responsibilities do they present to *you*—the American businessman—now and in years to come?" Accordingly, the presentation of the material here is divided into two parts: I—External Forces, and II—Internal Problems.

Attention is called to the fact that readers interested in following further any of the topics covered will find a bibliography, prepared by the Reference Department of Baker Library, Harvard Graduate School of Business Administration, at the end of the book.

The Editor has been given a free hand in organizing the various speeches, panel discussions, questions and answers, and observations —whose dynamic, spontaneous nature made them very effective orally—into an orderly, consistent form more suitable for reading. Accordingly, the identity of individual authors has been purposely subordinated. It should be made clear, however, that the views expressed in any chapter section are the responsibility of the specific author identified in the note at the beginning of the chapter, and as such are not necessarily representative of other authors or of the Harvard Business School Alumni Association.

Miss Virginia B. Fales and Miss Jane E. Hinchcliffe ably assisted in the editing.

Edward C. Bursk

August 27, 1951

CONTENTS

INTRODUCTION

Mobilizing Our Ideas and Ideals 3
Donald Kirk David

PART I: EXTERNAL FORCES

The Struggle for Men's Minds Abroad 13
Saville Davis, Raymond W. Miller, S. M. Jayanty, M. K. M. Lwin, J. U. Maegli, J. M. Nakpil, S. O. Ojo, A. S. Vassiliadis, and *Y. Takeno*

The Red Menace in Asia 37
Cornelio Balmaceda

An Economic Program for Asia 55
Raymond W. Miller and *C. Leigh Stevens*

The Atlantic Pact Nations 62
Thomas D. Cabot

Mobilization of Our Western Allies 69
N. E. Halaby, Colonel G. A. Lincoln, H. van Buren Cleveland, Ridgway B. Knight, and *Frederick Cone*

Relations with Latin America 89
Edward G. Miller, Jr.

PART II: INTERNAL PROBLEMS

The Problem of Inflation 101
Emerson P. Schmidt, Stanley H. Ruttenberg, and *David M. Wright*

Price and Wage Controls 123
Thomas L. Karsten, J. Keith Mann, and *Harold J. Walter*

MATERIALS CONTROLS 141

Horace B. McCoy, Malcolm Slaght, Frank Lewis, Edward J. Hanley, and *Eliot Janeway*

ORGANIZING PRODUCTION PERSONNEL 162

Franklin E. Folts, Roger Lowell Putnam, and *John D. Glover*

BUSINESS PROGRESS TOWARD STATESMANSHIP 180

Thomas D. Cabot, Horace N. Gilbert, Benjamin M. Selekman, George P. Baker, and *Stanley F. Teele*

SUPPLEMENT

THINKING AHEAD FOR BUSINESS—A SELECTED BIBLIOGRAPHY 205

Prepared by the Staff of Baker Library

INTRODUCTION

MOBILIZING OUR IDEAS AND IDEALS

Donald K. David

The decisions which businessmen make in the months ahead will determine largely whether we shall continue to advance toward or fall back from the positive goals which have made this country great. That is why we must "think ahead," as indicated by the title of this book.

Accordingly, in this introductory chapter, I should like to emphasize some of the ideas and ideals which must be kept in mind constantly while the immediate decisions are being made. If we should lose sight of our long-run goals under the pressure of our immediate problems, we could easily change the nature of our country and its future.

Perhaps today is a good time to appraise what has been done, in order that we may take account of ourselves. In our democratic way we seem to make progress by fits and starts. The swing of the pendulum determines our state of mind, and the pendulum seems to be controlled at the moment by the 38th parallel. We should not forget, though, that with each swing upward of the pendulum we do arrive at a new plateau, and one of our concerns should be to see that each time we keep the gains which we have achieved.

In the longer view, the crises we have faced together in the last thirty or forty years have intensified, strengthened, and helped define our goals. Two wars and a depression have brought us experiences which have made us realize our basic heritage. We, as pioneers, have always sought a positive goal and have been unafraid to state that goal in terms of the spiritual and moral values toward which we want to move. Though we know that we have never attained the goal completely, we have at least been able to measure whether we have been moving toward or retreating from it.

NOTE: Mr. David is Dean of the Harvard Graduate School of Business Administration.

Now we face another emergency. In facing this new crisis we must mobilize our ideas and ideals as well as our material resources. This is the positive way to insure continued progress toward our common goals.

But what can any of us do to contribute to this essential mobilization? I am convinced that for most of us the answer lies largely within the procedure of our normal occupations. Barbara Ward, the attractive and brilliant English writer, in her recent book, *Policy for the West,* uses two separate sentences which can serve as the framework for finding answers to our question: (1) "Unmobilized resources, however vast they may be, do not win wars." (2) "Never yet in human history has an ideal been defeated by no ideal at all."

Everyone knows that we have vast *material* resources, but there has been a commotion of discussion over what resources were needed, how many were available, how long we could stand a period of sustained mobilization, how much the people would be willing to sacrifice over a sustained period, and similar basic, practical questions. I do not claim to know the answers. But, as an illustration of certain answers that have been attempted, I should like to refer to an article, "Thinking Ahead," written by four Harvard Business School professors and signed by fourteen others.[1] In it are some estimates of what the United States economy could produce on a sustained basis of huge military preparations.

The authors conclude that the production capacity and man power of the United States are large enough to support armed forces of six million men and annual military expenditures of eighty-four billion dollars without "serious impairment" of the civilian economy, for as long a period as may prove to be necessary. This is significant when you realize that both the six million men and the eighty-four billion dollars were substantially higher than most public estimates made by our political leaders.

They also point out three of the major problems in "achieving preparedness to meet Russian aggression":

(1) They say it is "not merely a problem of having a given number of troops and quantity of weapons available at any moment,

[1] *Harvard Business Review,* vol. XXIX, no. 1 (January 1951), p. 119.

but of maintaining the basic capacity for whatever military operations may develop; nor is it so much a problem of peak effort and a swift culmination as of sustained readiness over a period of unknown and perhaps unknowable duration."

(2) They indicate that "we cannot concentrate solely on capacity to produce military end-items. We must also protect civilian morale and worker efficiency, which in turn imposes the requirement of maintaining our capacity to produce an adequate supply of civilian goods and services."

(3) They declare: "We must accomplish this high output of arms, this tolerable standard of living, and a steady flow of investment in new plant and equipment without running into a disastrous inflation. . . . [and] the resulting social strains and deterioration of moral fiber. To lose our economic health in order to achieve adequate preparedness would be tantamount to losing the main battle."

I would put their net conclusion in these words: The job can be done *if* we mobilize our ideas and ideals.

Important as is the mobilization of our economic and material resources, important as was the contribution made by these professors in trying to define the requirements more realistically and in bringing them to the public attention, they know and we all know it is not enough. It is not enough simply because it leaves unmobilized vast parts of our greatest resources—our ideals—and Barbara Ward's statement is just as true of moral, spiritual, and ideal strengths as it is of economic resources. "Unmobilized resources, however vast they may be, do not win wars."

I should like to make some positive suggestions for mobilizing these other resources. To begin with, we must sharpen our personal understanding of what our ideals are. Many of us are much clearer in our understanding of what we are *against* than what we are *for*. We need a positive program so that we, our people and others in the world, may have a clear picture of those things *for* which we stand. Some months ago I started for myself a little game—trying to list some things which, as I put it, were "as typical of the United States as the hot dog." I find it interesting and instructive to try to observe additional things to add to the list.

(1) I start with the right and opportunity of an individual to amount to something. Ideally, every individual should be able to amount to something—to the limit of his own merits, abilities, and ambition—unrestricted by class or artificial barriers such as race, color, creed, or economic position of his family. I say "ideally" because, as we all know, we can cite many instances where the ideal has not been achieved. For our purposes, however, the failure to attain perfection is not so important as the fact that the *ideal* exists and persists.

(2) I think we stand for a risk-taking, daring, venturesome climate. On all fronts—territorial, economic, artistic, in medicine, and even in sports, we have—at our best—stood for a creative, unafraid-to-try-the-new spirit. We have had the concept of fearless, dynamic pioneering. When the words "mature economy" crept into our vocabulary in the 1930's, something was happening to the country.

(3) The next idea I should like to mention grows quite naturally out of the first two: we have been brought up on the ideal and love of competition. As youngsters, not only did we take naturally to competitive sports, but our entire growing atmosphere organized the same lesson. School teams met with one another. From sand lot to Rose Bowl we competed on our playing fields; in our spelling bees and debates, our hog-calling contests, ski runs, professional sports, and even marathon dances. No wonder our elections are on a competitive basis. But our salvation is that we believe we should compete in a fair and sportsmanlike way: play the game hard, but fair.

(4) Our sales and marketing techniques have made possible a freedom for us, as individuals, to choose what we will or will not buy. It is interesting to note that in none of the writings of the leaders of Soviet thought, from Marx and Lenin to their current-day economists, are there references to the field of distribution or the science of marketing. I suspect that the development of our knowledge and skills in the area of distribution is the thing least understood or appreciated by our critics and may well prove to be the basic flaw in their arguments. I also believe that this freedom to choose what goods and services we will buy is one of the founda-

tion stones of many other freedoms and must, therefore, be carefully guarded.

There are of course more than these characteristics which are basic to our way of life. Our public school systems which are established to give additional meaning to the right of the individual to amount to something; the spirit of fair play which assures us protection and care of the aged, the infirm, the diseased, disabled, or deserted—these will suffice as illustrations of what I am trying to propose, if we remember that in our country they are all set in the framework of millions of centers of individual initiative. It is this fact which offers the opportunities necessary and makes it possible to preserve the freedom of choice so necessary to carrying out our goals.

Basically we want a positive kind of freedom: freedom for the individual to do things—freedom *to* rather than freedom *from.* In my opinion, the "freedom from want" and "freedom from fear" slogans are not basically consistent with our goals; our freedoms are better expressed in the freedom of the individual to make the most of himself. And the only negative part is that he be free from unfair interference from others who might hinder his ability to show what he can do. Thus it is that the traditional role of our government is to act as a referee—to see that no individual, in his own freedom *to,* unfairly interferes with another's freedom. Our government was not founded as a guarantor that everyone would be a winner.

No doubt each person has his own words for these ideals, for words are colored by the background of the person using them. Mine happen to be business-economic words. The churchman may emphasize the dignity of man. The statesman may use words similar to those in our own Declaration of Independence that "all men are endowed by their Creator with certain unalienable rights" and that "to secure these rights, governments are instituted among men, deriving their just powers from the consent of the governed." But no matter how you word it, these are the things we are really working for; these are the things we are really working *with.* These are the values we must maintain and strengthen, as we mobilize our economic strength.

Let me now be more specific with respect to what can be done by businessmen.

The complexities of our modern industrial society—mechanization of production; specialization and routinizing of jobs; four out of five people working for someone else; the growth of factories, corporations, and unions; and our greater interdependence one upon another—have thrown some serious roadblocks in the route toward the ideals I have mentioned. And business executives are right in the midst of the traffic jam. In my opinion, theirs is a great responsibility to devote themselves seriously to the task of seeing that individuals *do* have the opportunity to amount to something according to their abilities; that a risk-taking, daring, and venturesome climate *is* preserved and improved; and that they not only avoid standing in the way but take positive steps to assure the continuation of competition, hard but fair.

There are some who warn businessmen that if they fail to do these things, their right to be businessmen will be taken away. I believe that this negative attitude, this threatening motivation, is neither necessary nor likely to succeed. Businessmen have been recognizing this problem more and more and are learning how to deal with it under normal competitive situations. They have begun to draw effectively upon the skills of those outside business, such as our universities, psychologists, sociologists, students of administration, and the like. As I see it, by their right actions businessmen not only can fulfill our economic needs but can contribute quite as much, if not more than any other group toward the effective mobilization of our common ideals and ideas, both for sustained readiness and long-run welfare.

We are all aware that throughout the history of our country there were some who thought our progress must end as one frontier after another disappeared. When we had all but conquered our territorial frontiers, there were some unimaginative people who thought our growth was over; but, science, technology, and, yes, business created new frontiers which raised our physical standards of living to heights the early pioneers had never thought possible. Now these frontiers have been pushed so far that some fearful people believe not only that progress must stop, but that we have created a Frankenstein which will destroy us. As I see it, however, if we recapture, cling to, and accelerate our traditional approach toward ideals and human values, precisely the opposite can be true. A new frontier to conquer is opening up before us—the frontier of knowledge of human and administrative affairs—a frontier, like the others before it, filled with opportunity whereby we can push ahead still further toward our basic ideals and make them more of a reality.

Cautious persons may urge prudence, may suggest not probing the new frontier until the emergency is passed. To this I cannot in honesty agree, for the simple reason that what lies beyond that frontier is both what we are fighting *with* and what we are fighting *for*. The more we learn about it now, the better chance we have to win and the better chance we have to have something worthwhile after victory.

True, we shall have to postpone some of the long-run explorations of the frontier; we shall have to adjust our immediate sights somewhat. But I believe we must move on; that each of us individually can determine the part we should play; and that if we are true to our ideals and each and every one of us makes the effort, we shall succeed.

PART I

EXTERNAL FORCES

THE STRUGGLE FOR MEN'S MINDS ABROAD

Saville Davis, Raymond W. Miller, S. M. Jayanty, M. K. M. Lwin, J. U. Maegli, J. M. Nakpil, S. O. Ojo, A. S. Vassiliadis, and Y. Takeno

INTRODUCTION

There are, it seems to me, two enormous gaps that we face in the world today.

The first is the tremendous gap in the factual knowledge which we and other people have of each other. I have come across striking examples of it in talking with people from other lands when I try to look at the United States through their eyes.

We are an economically advanced country, which in some respects is culturally backward, and they are the reverse.

We are a country which is in a strong upsurge of free enterprise. Many of the other countries are partly so, but only partly so, such as some of the more advanced countries in Europe; the rest, those that are less developed, are in a stage of much more government control, or semisocialism, if you wish to call it that. These undeveloped countries are trying to pull themselves up by their bootstraps, trying to lift themselves up into the modern age and leap whole generations in a short time. They often honestly believe they cannot do it without methods which we would reject as being bad.

Right there is the conflict to which we have to adjust ourselves. We feel that they are hostile to free enterprise in many respects;

NOTE: Mr. Davis is American News Editor, *Christian Science Monitor;* Mr. Miller is Consultant to the Food and Agriculture Organization, United Nations; Mr. Jayanty (India), Mr. Lwin (Burma), Mr. Maegli (Guatemala), Mr. Nakpil (Philippines), Mr. Ojo (Nigeria), and Mr. Vassiliadis (Greece) are students at the Harvard Graduate School of Business Administration; Mr. Takeno is Chief of the Repatriation Section of the Japanese Foreign Office.

This chapter is based on a discussion in which all the authors participated informally. As presented here, the introduction and conclusion are drawn from the observations of Mr. Miller and Mr. Davis; the geographical sections reflect the views of the individual men representing the various countries.

they feel, even now, in spite of everything else, that we are on an imperialistic bent when we consider making investments in their countries, and that we will interfere with their lives in a way which is unacceptable to them.

The first thing that we should do is to try to arrive at a better understanding of what these countries think of the United States.

The other gap, equally serious, is a technical one.

On the one side is the need for development programs across the world. We must bring the undeveloped countries up to the level of the modern era; otherwise we perish. There is such massed impatience on the part of these people that if we cannot provide the better standards of living they see others enjoy, they will turn to Russia to get what they want more quickly.

On the other side, there is the kind of talk which goes on when American businessmen sit down together, about the investment of capital under tolerable, safe terms. How can we go into these countries and make investments, or form partnership arrangements, and still protect our capital and our stockholders from all the hazards and the uncertainties, the nationalism and the political revolutions, and the like?

Somehow we must bridge the gap between the need of the undeveloped countries and the willingness and ability at the present time of American businessmen and investors to make a specific effort to try to resolve that need.

We, as citizens of the world, are engaged today in the most colossal struggle for the control of men's thinking that the world has ever seen. We have had in the past, back through the centuries, influences that affected various groups or sections of the world. There was the Renaissance in Europe: that set out to control men's minds. There was the Reformation in Europe: that had certain things to do with the control of men's minds. There was the Prophecy and the working out of the Prophet, Mohammed, in Asia: that had much to do with influencing men's minds.

In the meantime, Christianity had come out of the East and spread over Europe; it took a race of savages and changed them to the modern Europeans. I sometimes wonder what would have happened if Christianity had gone south, in the other direction, for at no time did it come smack up against the whole world.

Today we are in a situation where the overwhelming majority of the men and women in the world are cognizant of the fact that there is a drive on to influence their thinking. The drive is concentrated, on one side, in what I define as despotic, materialistic imperialism and, on the other side, in the free world, free enterprise, the things that stand for the liberty of men's minds.

But there is an old rule which has come out of the schools of theology: that man is much more influenced by what goes into his stomach and by what goes on his back than he is by the spirit, until such time as his stomach is full or his back is covered.

You can send speakers into the Far East to talk on the glories of private enterprise, but that kind of preaching falls flat, because the average person does not understand what is being discussed; he is hungry, and when men are hungry, how can they be interested in something like private enterprise?

On the other hand, I heard a speech two years ago in India by a representative of Soviet Russia. It was one of the most effective speeches I have ever heard a man make in my life. He swept the crowd off their feet. His story was very simple. He said that they had tried Christianity and capitalism in Russia for three hundred or four hundred years, and the net result of these attempts was illiteracy, poverty, disease; and he said that now, for a period of a generation, they had tried another system; and he went on to relate the wonderful things that happened. Now whether he was right or whether he was lying is beside the point. He influenced the crowd; he influenced men's minds.

I was in Hong Kong not long ago—the only city in the world that I know of where the East and the West completely mix. The people on the other side of the Iron Curtain and those on our side of the Curtain are completely separated, but twenty-five thousand women go back and forth each day. And there you can see this thing that we are talking about—this matter of influences on people's minds, out of which the future of the world will be shaped.

Notice that I said twenty-five thousand women. Major General

F. L. Brayne of the British Army (retired), one of the greatest Christian statesmen I ever met, who spent forty years in India and ten years in the rest of the Far East, says that, in his opinion, if we are going to influence the world, to save it from suicide, we must begin by influencing the thinking of the women of the world. He despairs of men having much to do with saving the world. And, maybe he is right! The average woman in the undeveloped parts of this world has very little chance to be anything but one of three things: a plaything of a man, a bearer of children, a beast of burden. In the minds of such women there is welling up a desire for something different, something better. I agree with the General: that is what primarily is putting the impetus behind this surge toward the materialistic despotism of Central Asia.

To summarize: in the battle for men's minds throughout the world we have got to approach people on the level on which they live, not on the high levels of the glories of capitalism and the glories of private enterprise. That will come later.

We have got to take care of the food, clothing, and housing first.

For the moment, the most important thing to remember is that we cannot sell words or propaganda; we will be judged, in the parts of the world where they suspect us, not by words and propaganda but by specific actions. Let me give you an example of what can be done:

> The Philippine city of Sabu was one of the most bombed places in the world, for it was bombed by the American bombers to get rid of the enemy. It was absolutely a shambles. Into that city moved a young man by the name of Pedro. He was a graduate of the University of Washington (I call him Pedro Ph.D.), and he got his degree by washing dishes and by working on the salmon run. He desired to put the idea of democracy to work. He wanted to influence the minds of these men and women in the collapsed city—that is exactly what it was—to seek a better world. What happened? In a period of two and a half years' time he and his wife organized Parent-Teachers groups and Boy Scouts, and they built eight hundred school buildings, built them from scratch. And the American businessmen in that city (glory to them!) went out and helped.

Sabu is today the focal point in the Philippines of the drive for democracy. Here there is complete understanding of this thing that we call democracy. Here democracy is succeeding. Why? Because the battle for men's minds was on a level that the people understood —their wants and needs—and because it was fought with deeds not words.

Now let us look at the situation in several representative countries.

The Philippines

According to the Bell Report,[1] the problems of the Philippines could be summarized under three main headings:

(1) Inefficient production and very low incomes of the people.
(2) The increasingly critical condition of government finances.
(3) Serious distortion of the international payment position of the country (the balance has been maintained only by import and exchange controls).

The causes of these difficulties are the following:

(1) There has been no increase in the productive efficiency, and the economy is not diversified enough.
(2) Investments have been misdirected, and there have been excessive imports.
(3) A dangerous inflationary condition has resulted from large budgetary deficiencies and excessive creation of credit by the government and government-controlled corporations.
(4) Foreign investments have been discouraged by the unfavorable economic and political environment and by the fear of discrimination.
(5) The economy shows little inherent capacity to overcome difficulties because of the widespread feeling of disillusion. The workers have no faith that the position can be improved, and the businessmen fear a collapse of the peso. There is also a recent tendency toward unemployment, resulting in the slow-up of construction and the sharp curtailment of imports.

Those are the basic difficulties and the causes for these difficulties as found by the Bell Report.

There are seven points recommended by the Bell Report:

(1) The placing of government finances on a sound basis by additional tax revenues, including (a) revision of the present tax structures

[1] *Report to the President of the United States by the Economic Survey Mission to the Philippines* (Washington, Government Printing Office, 1950).

and the overhauling of the tax-collecting machinery; (b) adoption of a credit policy which would encourage investment in productive enterprises, and (c) coördination of fiscal, credit, and investment policy, to prevent inflation. (The addition of tax revenues has been already adopted by the Philippine Congress, and the Philippine Government is beginning to take action along the lines recommended.)

(2) The improvement of agricultural production, including (a) supplying the Department of Agriculture with enough funds to rehabilitate the government agricultural colleges, (b) establishment of more rural banks for the credit facilities of the farmers in the country, and (c) expediting the opening of new lands for settlements and homesteads, redistribution of lands through purchase of large estates for resale to small farmers, and providing tenants with reasonable security and an equitable share of crops.

(3) The diversification of the economy by encouraging new industries.

(4) The levy of a special 25 per cent emergency tax, for a two-year period, on imports other than rice, corn, flour, canned milk, fish, and fertilizer; the reëxamination of the trade agreement with the United States; and the imposition of a 25 per cent sales tax on sales of exchange.

(5) The establishment of an adequate program of public health and improved education, to be undertaken by the Philippine Government, and the building of better facilities for urban housing for the people.

(6) The improvement and reorganization of public administration so as to insure honesty, efficiency, and good officers in the government.

(7) The provision of financial assistance of two hundred and fifty million dollars through loans and grants from the United States, to help carry out the five-year program of economy development and provide the necessary technical assistance. This aid is strictly conditioned on steps being taken by the Philippine Government to carry out the other suggestions recommended by the Bell Commission under the supervision and control of a United States Technical Commission.

If I may try to summarize, this amounts to an over-all program, very comprehensive in its scope, which provides that the Philippines themselves take certain steps, A, B, C, D, and so on; and that, after those steps are initiated, then a system of loans can be put into operation to finance them.

This leads to the question of the interference by the United States in the affairs of the Philippines. Do the Philippine people want it and like it? And further, if it is interference, what can be done to minimize the interference?

I believe that it is not any form of interference at all. Of course it depends on one's point of view. I would rather look at it as a safeguard for the money that will be invested by the American Government in the Philippines, in the form of loans and grants.

There are people, to be sure, especially those who have a tendency to lean toward the left, who look at this as a form of imperialism, as more or less a kind of compulsion on the Philippines to do whatever the American Government would like them to do.

The Communists have been making as much capital out of that idea as possible, but most of the recommendations of the Bell Report, so far as the tax structure revisions are concerned, have been adopted by the Philippine Government, as I have stated previously. For example, the 25 per cent excise tax on the sale of exchange has been adopted.

I would say that the economic background of the Philippines, just before we got our independence, was most inopportune. We got our independence after the war, in 1946, when the country was down and out. In spite of that, however, I believe that we have the physical and the human resources in the country which, together with the aid from the United States, will carry us on.

So far as the success of the Communists in the Philippines is concerned, I might say that they have had to resort to forcing their ideas by means of arms. Right now we do not deal with the Communists by speaking to them. I mean by this that things have gone so far that we are shooting at each other.

Most of the Communists' followers are illiterate farmers whom they have conscripted and forced to work for them, whereas most of the Communist leaders—eight or ten of them who direct the others from the mountains—are extremely well educated. Even with the use of force the Communists have few followers in the cities. By and large the people in the cities are the foremost exponents of democracy in the Far East; they serve as an example that it can work.

Burma

Burma faces another kind of situation than does the Philippines, and the Bell Report recommendations would not be applicable there because of the difference between its administrative structure and that of the Philippines. In Burma there is a Socialistic form of government, whereas the Philippine form of government is more like that of the United States.

Burma went through a period when there were a number of pro-Communists in power. The explanation for that situation lies in the conditions that existed during the previous regimes—for instance, the way a farmer had to live from year to year.

The typical farmer—a tenant farmer, unable to get ahead and save—was always in need of working capital and for most of the year dependent on purchased food. He got the foodstuffs from the village shops on credit and subsequently paid for them out of his crops. Under this system of credit, for instance, he might have to pay back one hundred baskets of rice at harvest time for the thirty baskets of rice he had received—in other words, interest of over 300 per cent for a term of only four to six months—a very typical situation. To get his working capital for the year, he would go to his landlord (usually a foreigner). Then for the rainy season, before harvest time, he might need money again and borrow it from the landlord. These loans would be paid back in what he produced at the end of the harvest, leaving the farmer destitute for another year.

Under that situation, the farmers have been, in fact, enslaved by those people who own the capital. As for the workers in the mines and public utilities, which are mostly owned by British businessmen, virtually the same thing applies to them.

Though this kind of exploitation has been practiced by local Burmese landlords too, 75 per cent of the land is owned by foreigners—English and Indians, with the latter in the great majority. The preponderance of Indians is explained by the fact that Burma was a part of India until 1935; indeed, Indians have been settled in Burma for nearly two centuries. When Burma got its independence in 1948 along with India, the Burmese Government wanted the Indians to go back home, particularly those Indians who had a large supply of funds at their disposal and who were doing a money-lending business. But the trouble was that the farmers who were cultivating the land needed to borrow money and had nowhere else to turn. Perhaps we should say that it is not the landowners but the system that is basically at fault.

Of course, attempts have been made to correct the situation. The Burmese Government introduced a land-requisitioning program whereby the land could be purchased back from the Indian landlords. But the government is still arguing with the landlords about the price and the terms for the purchase of the land. So even now the Communist idea of confiscating lands appears quite attractive to the young nationalists and political leaders. The Communists distributed much literature about the economic situation of the country to the students and the younger politicians and the nationalists, and it was studied enthusiastically.

To reach the workers on the land, the Communists have sometimes worked through already-existing farmers' organizations; usually, however, the Communists are trained to organize local groups themselves and are directed to do so by their party.

The government, soon after the country secured its independence, was very much in favor of the Communist way of doing things. There are still some Communists and pro-Communists in the Burmese Government at the present time. After about two years of experience with Communism, however, most of the government officials have changed their minds. For example, they tried to nationalize the inland waterways—the British-owned transportation system—and they played with the problem of electing technicians and experienced men. But the operation broke down because they were faced with a deficit. As a matter of fact, at one time there was not enough cash to pay the salaries of the employees because of the inefficient management by the government.

There is a difference between the American and the Russian ways of winning people's minds. The Americans in Burma tried to approach the people as a whole by showing them pictures of America, telling them about the American standard of living, and advocating liberty, freedom, and free enterprise. But the Communists just concentrated on the individuals who took part in the political groups, such as the students, the clubs, or the teachers. They would form a little society and organize discussion groups where they studied

Communist literature (translated into Burmese). Through the younger politicians and the nationalists, who became enthused about Communism, they thus transmitted their ideologies to the rest of the population.

People are not inclined to believe foreigners talking about a foreign country. (The fact is that Americans are talking about America, generally. And what do they say? Nothing! Propaganda, and lies too. For Americans are not really enjoying such high standards of living.) But when the local leaders who hold the Communist theories preach Communism, the people in general are inclined to believe what they say. Certainly this Russian method of approach through the proper channels—the groups of people who have influence on the rest of the masses of the people—is much more effective than the American propaganda approach.

Of course, when it comes to the matter of capital investment, the Burmese Government would not be averse to aid from the Americans. (Certainly they would favor aid from the Americans more than from the British, because they have had unhealthy relations with the British Government for a hundred years, and the Burmese people are rather prejudiced against the British Government.) But in any event the Burmese would wish to keep control of any cooperative investment arrangements in Burma, say, on a basis of 51 per cent Burmese and 49 per cent foreign.

India

Although we are interested in foreigners' investing in India, the government is not prepared to extend any special invitation to any country. The reason is that the Indian Government is reluctant to advance any special economic assistance which the investors might ask for. If they want to come to India and invest money, they have got to work alongside Indian capitalists, with the same privileges, the same obligations, the same risks. In most cases, they should be operating not only on equal terms with the Indian capitalists, who own most of the industries there, but actually they must operate within similar organizations.

India welcomes capital from the outside, working with and through Indian industry in coöperative arrangements—perhaps on a 51–49 basis. But note that India wants to have the control. It does not want the foreigners to take all the profits, as the British have been doing for so many years, not only in India but in Iran. Nevertheless, India is not going to harm foreign investors in any way, and their interests will be absolutely safe. India expects to nationalize the basic industries and the production of power. Beyond that, there will be no interference; all other industries will operate in the same way that they are now.

We need roads, schools, hospitals, public sanitation, and irrigation systems; and these are not things which can be built by the free-enterprise system of America, as I see it. I believe there is little room for free enterprise before these things are accomplished.

But India is not altogether a backward country, either in agriculture or industry. It does not lack resources for development, although in the early stages of building the economy, it may have to look to the West for technical aid. Not only can the United States give us the technical aid we need, but perhaps it can also give us the machinery for which we cannot really pay in dollars.

I certainly do not think that the United States has failed in the other countries where it has spent money. The Marshall Plan has achieved its objectives. But the Marshall Plan, so far as I know, has been extended only to the European countries, where billions of dollars have been spent. In contrast, the Point Four Program, which is supposed to help build the underdeveloped countries, after a great fight in the United States Congress over ten million dollars, amounts to only thirty-four million dollars. That is just a drop in the ocean, so far as we see it; in fact, it looks to some like eyewash.

The Marshall Plan aid has been used for rebuilding the European standard of living, which is already far beyond the Asiatics'. What is worse, at the very time that Britain, France, Denmark, and other European countries are being fed by American aid, they have been pursuing ruthless colonial policies in Africa. The Indonesians are fighting for their independence; yet the French got help to shoot down the Indochinese and Malayans. And I have read somewhere that the Belgians still treat the Africans as slaves in the Belgian Congo.

Can anyone, especially Americans, look at the facts and deny that the United States is not unselfish in extending help and aid to other countries? Certainly the Marshall aid is looked upon to some extent as an aid to putting countries on their feet, but is it merely coincidental that by extending such aid the United States has also obtained bases in Europe from which to strike Russia? Well, India has little to offer in that direction, although India is as much opposed to Communism and the Russian-inspired Communist Party as other nations are. It took the United States five months to grant food to India—on a loan basis, at that. Why? Because India wants to retain its liberty in its own way.

All these facts have to some extent caused the Indians to form an adverse opinion of the United States and its real intentions.

Greece

Greece is in a different category from the countries just discussed, as there is ample capital that has not been invested and is not being invested at the present time. The trouble is that those who have the potential investment money fear very much that what happened in the last war is going to happen all over again; i.e., that just about the time they get something started, another war will break out and their plants will be destroyed by bombing. Or, if that does not happen, they fear that the Communists will take over in Greece, and that those who have been tagged as capitalists will be liquidated. So no one wants to build up a name as owning such-and-such an enterprise or such-and-such a plant.

Here is a case of needing to induce the Greek capitalists to go ahead and build plants and invest money in various enterprises, and so on, rather than seeking foreign investment money. Even when those who have the potential capital—and, as I have said, there is plenty of it—put their money into enterprises that will bring back the initial investment in a comparatively short time, they hesitate to go any further. This tendency has been particularly pronounced since the Korean war started. Before that, there was a considerable resurgence of activity; people had started working again, industry was moving, and plants were producing. But with the beginning of the Korean war and the ensuing international crises, all this activity just died out.

This situation illustrates the tremendous difficulty of organizing any kind of international program for industrial development, and for improving the economic status of people generally, at a time when they are subject to all the hazards of fear and the uncertainties of the international struggle for power.

All this points up the question of foreign investment. Is there not some other way to help countries? Certainly just hit-or-miss investing is not the wisest way to do it.

The English were in Greece when we were having a Communist uprising. They tried to help us by bringing in troops to fight the Communists. That only aggravated matters. After two years they had to leave Greece. Then the Americans came in—Van Fleet and others—and brought technical assistance and advice. Soon the Communist revolution was stopped.

Not only is technical assistance, applied in a businesslike way, the most efficient method of providing help, but it also does not cost the United States very much. And, further, we in the other countries would not be always hearing from our American friends: "Oh, you live off the ECA."

There is much potential power within the people of Europe. They have a lot of spirit that they can put to good use. Other people have done it. I am thinking of the example of Sabu that was mentioned earlier; the Philippine people built something out of nothing, out of their own resources. Also I recall what I have heard about the achievements in Israel; those people, too, started from almost nothing. It is more than just a matter of money. The dollar sign is the result, not the cause of success. The conviction that people want to work and want to produce and improve is the important fundamental principle of any reconstruction program.

I believe that if America sends technical experts who will work along with the governments or with individual businessmen in developing ideas and carrying them out, magnificent results can be achieved. Let me give you a good example. We had in the area around Athens a whole section of land that was all marshes and swampland; nobody ever touched it. But we managed, with technical advice and expert help, to reclaim it; and now it has turned out to be one of the most fertile rice-producing pieces of land in the world.

Here is an example on the other side—what happens when a different course is followed. I am referring to the way the Americans came into Greece with their arms loaded with goods, thinking that by giving things away they were helping the people. For instance, they noticed that some of the Greek people were barefooted. So they decided to bring in shoes, and they have been bringing in shoes and shoes and shoes for years now. Well, that has resulted in the closing down of the tanneries in Greece, one of our most vital industries.

Again, the main product of Greece for export is tobacco. Our chief market used to be Germany. But the Americans went in there with their Lucky Strikes, Camels, and Chesterfields; the Germans began smoking the American cigarettes; and now they do not want to buy Greek tobacco any more.

And so I believe that it is not a matter of looking at individual interests in the individual countries; it is a matter of looking at the whole world as an entity and trying, through technical assistance and advice, to come to a focal point of balancing production.

For instance, if we break down the economic and political boundaries between countries, if the Schuman Plan is extended to a larger number, and if the United States of Europe ever comes close to achievement, that will be the key to success. As it is now, the markets are so limited that high prices have to be set on the goods, and those high prices mean that very few people can buy. That is why we have a few people who can afford everything and the masses of the people who cannot afford to buy anything.

Therefore, if we could manage to make more goods available to everybody through specialization of the industries in the various countries, and could increase the exports and imports, I think that

that would be one of the most efficient ways of attaining prosperity and avoiding the excess expenditures and risks of investment.

Nigeria

Nigeria is one of the two African states evolving democratic governments on the west coast of Africa; the other is Liberia. When President Truman announced the Point Four Program, we were very happy about it, and we expected to have experts to help us with our reforms, both agricultural and economic. But, up to the present time at least, it appears that the South American countries and Liberia are the people who are deriving the benefits from the Point Four Program, and that makes us think that perhaps the program was meant for those countries whose economies are closely tied in with that of the United States.

Now, it may be surprising to know how jealous some people are. We are jealous, and we still expect that the United States will help us with technical advice and agricultural aid in the form of tractors and dairy equipment. Perhaps it will also be surprising to know that for the first time in our history our city population starved this year. We are concerned about that, and we still are looking to America to help us develop our economy.

Another thing which bothers us is that, in the Eastern Hemisphere, American attention seems to be directed solely toward Asia. In this connection, I think that it is very important to realize that Nigeria, like Liberia, is led by Americans as well as by Africans; that although we have suffered under the British in the past, we have not yet had any Communists; and that the type of democratic government which we are evolving promises to be a relatively stable one. There is no likelihood of a civil war; we hope that we are going to be able to achieve our goal within five or ten years by peaceful means. In other words, foreign investment will be safe with us, because we are not fanatics.

As for the question of how Americans should extend capital outside, without danger of appropriation by the country in which the capital is being used, I agree with what Mr. Edward Miller says in his discussion. The best way by which capital could flow from the developed areas to the underdeveloped areas is to make the capital represent the national life of the place where it operates.

But always remember that the people in our area do not pay too much attention to money. We are not concerned with the amount of profits a company makes as much as we are with the kind of "human relations" it has. Are as many of our own people employed as possible—both skilled and unskilled? Do the investors or their representatives identify themselves with the natives, so that we have the feeling that the enterprise is our own rather than belonging primarily to foreigners? Are these outsiders arrogant—if you will excuse the name-calling—like some others we have had experience with? When people say, "Well, I worked with that man, and he treated me like a dog," it does not take a day before public opinion is against his company; and in a democracy the government represents the common people.

American companies can operate through subsidiaries in underdeveloped areas just as they do in Canada, in England, and elsewhere. But they must make some modifications; they must go out of their way to use as much of the native labor as possible and to select management representatives who will be able to identify themselves with the natives. Those are important clues to the way in which capital should be extended from a developed area to underdeveloped areas.

I would like to add a few points on how American people have failed to reach the masses of the people in the outside world. To my mind, it is a serious omission that they do not go through the proper local channels. When Americans are in a foreign-speaking city, they usually associate themselves with the British (or sometimes French) officials—and those men just are not popular in Nigeria. The man in the street, meeting an American who asks a question showing ignorance of Nigeria, is immediately suspicious. This American has been staying with the English and taking tea with them; obviously he has failed to talk to the native people.

In a society where there are not very many people who can read and where there are few discussion groups, there is only one effective channel of communication—hearsay, from mouth to mouth. That is why the United States should work in Nigeria through the native people—through their own organizations and their own elected officials.

Actually, it is not difficult to talk to the native people. America, particularly, is very lucky, in that the educated people in West Africa are all American-educated. I remember well one American, Mr. Munger, who showed extremely good sense in staying in one of our native homes. In this way he became acquainted with all the chiefs and also the local people. When I met him, he immediately knew about my town. This indication that he had a good knowledge of the different parts of the country naturally made a favorable impression.

The American missionaries in West Africa represent another group of people through whom American businessmen can work. They are loved and respected because they help the people—adopt orphan children and all sorts of things like that. So when the Americans come into our country with the "Voice of America," instead of associating with the British or the French, they should live with the missionaries or stay with one of the educated natives. I know that I will be ready to accommodate any American businessman who wants to visit me when I go back home, and thousands of my countrymen are willing to do the same thing.

Guatemala

I do not agree that the United States Government must of course bring American businessmen to the realization that they need to invest in Latin American countries. For they should already know that. By investing in our countries they will (1) secure raw materials, (2) create a market for their products, and (3) build up a middle class, an industrial middle class, such as is lacking in our countries at the present time. The Guatemalan population, for example, is made up largely of Indians, with a small group of landowners. What we need is a strong middle class to stabilize our politics.

American companies have been willing to invest several million dollars in our country, just in exploring it, which means a lot to us. But the Guatemalan Government has a narrow view and is shortsighted too. It deals in symbols. It thinks that the Americans are going to exploit us, so it has not given the American companies a fair opportunity.

The potential oil production in Guatemala is a particularly sore subject. I believe that we should give the opportunity for investment in oil to that company that gives us the best deal, and we should let it operate our oil industry. We do not have the capital to do it ourselves. My government would be in favor of a 51–49 arrangement in the development of the oil resources. But I am afraid that the Americans distrust us. Perhaps we would have to give them a 50–50 arrangement.

I feel very strongly about the investment matter. All the Americas need United States investment, just as the United States needs our raw materials. (I think it was Nelson Rockefeller who pointed out that 73 per cent of six critical raw materials came from the undeveloped areas.) So I have tried, in the three or four years that I have been in the United States, to talk to as many businessmen as I could to find out how interested their companies were in investing in Latin America. The response that I have always gotten is, "Well, you know, we had our fingers burned in the 1920's."

Rockefeller, I think, is about the most farsighted businessman who has gone into Latin America, Brazil, and Ecuador since the war. In 1949 he invested seven million dollars there. Though he is still not breaking even, he is close to doing so. His organization is the International Basic Economy Corporation (IBEC)—a nonprofit affiliate. The IBEC has gone into both the distribution systems and the farming systems of the countries on a 50–50 basis, with the idea, first of all, of giving the local people a break. These ventures are underwritten on an amortization basis.

It is important to realize that Latin Americans definitely have different ideas about business from those of North Americans. We, for example, consider friendship among businessmen equally as important as business itself. I would say that there is a tendency toward distrusting anybody who comes into the country just to do business.

This is important, for it is a basic attitude. Our businessman says to himself, "Here comes an American. He wants to make a fast 'buck' as he did in the twenties." There is a prejudicial attitude on both sides. We must develop basic understanding. If we do, I am sure we can find a great many honest people with whom to deal on both sides.

I might add something about the way to sell the United States to Latin America. The way to start is with the realization that basically the United States system does not work in our country. We are quite different; we have our own traditions. Then the thing to do is to try to get the United States accepted as a friend, a positive friend, and not just as the lesser of two evils (the other being Communism).

It is not easy to convince the people of just what Russia truly is and does—for example, that in Russia they put people in concentration camps. Many a time I have faced the Communists in Italy, or in Guatemala, or other places, and I have said to them, "Do you believe that there are slave workers in Russia?" And they have said, "No; that's a dirty lie."

Well, how are you going to demonstrate the basic truth to the people—which is what you have to do? Only by comparing the two systems and making a pro-and-con analysis of what the workers are really faced with, can you get anywhere. It is not enough just to say, "We do it this way," or, "We do it that way." It is not enough to use propaganda or pressure. Nothing will do but to set forth the facts and give the people their choice.

Not that this will be easy. I have lived in the United States for six years, and I think that I have acquired a broader view than most of my countrymen have. But I cannot forget how the three big United States companies we have down there (the United Fruit Company, the railroad company, and the main electrical and power company) got into the country under extremely favorable concessions—others, less charitable, might say by "shady dealings" or, in other words, by bribing the local politicians. Consequently these companies—along with the United States as a whole—have quite a past to live down.

I might say that the United Fruit Company, right now, is paying the best agricultural salaries in the country. But the politicians will not let the people forget what the United Fruit Company used to do in the past. They think in symbols—in this case, the symbol of American business, big business, or, as Communist propaganda puts it, Wall Street business.

The only other United States representatives that we see are the tourists. About the only thing they ever say to us is "Oh, my goodness, but you have houses here, too!" or "Let me take your picture."

Now, perhaps, that is an exaggerated generalization for the whole United States as a whole, but, exaggerated or not, it indicates a dangerous sort of relationship. You do not get close to the people that way, and you only create prejudices.

I have been faced with these things at college and even in school. Almost eight times out of ten, when I say I am from Guatemala, I have been confronted with a puzzled look on the faces of my fellow schoolmates; I can almost hear them thinking, "Just where in South America is this country of his?" as they try in vain to remember their last geography course, which of course they took in the primary schools.

I think that right here, on this simple point, there has to be a complete change in attitude. We want to understand you, and we need to understand you. You also need to understand us. Maybe you had better begin by learning, first of all, where we are located; then, just who we are, what we want, what we think, and what our history is.

Japan

Frankly speaking, the Japanese people received the American occupation people in much fear. We did not expect a generous or lenient attitude. But now, and indeed for two years or more, the sentiments on the part of the Japanese people have completely changed. We have come to respect the occupation forces, because the occupation authorities have done so much to deserve our respect.

At the time of the surrender, our national life was desperate; our families, personally speaking, were on the verge of starvation;

clothes and food were very scarce. Up to now, if I am not mistaken, twenty million dollars at least has been given to the Japanese for reconstruction in various fields, and we are grateful for this help and assistance.

The Japanese people are really repentant about what they did in the war. We have made up our minds to reconstruct our country in a more respectable direction. We have worked hard—and our people are industrious, as you may know, for you must be studious and industrious to feed eighty-three million people in a country that is smaller than California.

As to the question of land reforms, previously much of rural Japan—especially in the northern part—was occupied by big landholding families, with their tenants or peasants still at the feudal stage, unable to make complaints against their landlords. But now, with the coming of Allied personnel, we are making large-scale land reforms.

I am going to confine these remarks to rural Japan because it constitutes the bulk of the Japanese population.

Sixty technicians went out into the countryside within two days following the landing of the military forces. Note these facts: (1) They carried no arms. (2) They immediately went to work with the Japanese people. (3) They were the ordinary, run-of-the-mill people; one of them was an attorney for the Farm Coöperatives in Minnesota, and one of them was a Professor of Geology at Stanford.

These men lived with the Japanese people, and they tried to demonstrate to them that Japan could pull itself up by its bootstraps by taking the technical information from abroad and applying it on a democratic basis, in its own way. At no time did these technicians attempt at all to impose America on Japan, but gave the Japanese people an opportunity to take what they already had and use it to better advantage.

Let me give you a concrete example of the results achieved as I saw them in the rural communities and the fishing communities. Take the fishing communities of Japan alone. There are about twelve thousand communities in Japan that are utterly dependent upon fish for their living. Most of them are isolated. They had been subject for centuries to the thing that has been described as feudalism. Three of the American technicians went in there and began working with the Japanese people to show them that the fish in the sea might be made available for the people of the area in a way that would bring prosperity to all concerned.

They really helped the fishermen. They organized more than ten thousand community coöperatives. These little coöperatives now take the fish produced by the small people, mass them together, and ship them to Tokyo and other places. Naturally, the fishermen are receiving greater returns.

There are several further advantages to these community coöperatives. For one thing, they make credit available on reasonable terms. (In this they are similar to the credit unions which have been introduced in India from America.) For another thing, they make the Japanese people feel that they are participants.

Whether the thing would operate as well without a military mandate, I do not know. MacArthur used the Potsdam Declaration, as it was once called; he clamped down and said that this must be tried out. After that, he allowed the Japanese to follow through, and the Japanese Diet took appropriate action.

It is my personal opinion that in most of the Asiatic countries, the United States, to be successful, should, first of all, send in representatives who would live with the people or the missionaries. (Let me say that I agree with the point made earlier about the missionaries.) It does not matter what denomination—Protestant, Catholic, or Apostolic Holy Rollers. The missionaries out in the field are the men who are known and loved in Asia.

And next in order, the best representatives are the technicians. As an example of that second point, let me say that the FAO of the United Nations has recently sent 140 technicians to Asia and to South America, and three have gone to Africa to live with the people and to take information to them.

To sum up, the monetary assistance given us has contributed to reconstruction and maintenance of economic stability. The technical assistance has been even more important in the sense that it is more fundamental; it serves to guide us to do things correctly and properly in the future. And, perhaps most significant of all, during the occupation we have learned a lot about moral principles in daily life, and we have especially welcomed many of the missionary people.

I think that if our people had more chances to come over here to America and learn, as I have, it would be lucky for the Japanese people in the rebuilding of their future. In my own experience during the short time that I have been here, one of the first things I have learned is that you have creative power—the most creative power—in many fields. The Japanese are noted for imitation. But this time—I want your forgiveness—we want to imitate that creative power!

Conclusion

It is rather disillusioning to a great many of us, no doubt, to have some of these realities brought out. However, I should like to advance the theory that we cannot solve anything by ignoring it.

Let us admit that one of the main reasons why Communism has been making such progress abroad is that a great deal of what Communists say about capitalism is true; it has been exploiting the masses for profit to a few in too many cases. We do not get very far by telling the local people in South America or Asia that we want to help them when they know perfectly well that the help is going to disappear along the way in the pockets of a certain class of businessmen who have never considered that they owe anything to their country—or to anyone but themselves.

What we need is more enlightened management of investment abroad. The question of the 51–49 arrangement as an alternative to the 50–50 arrangement has been brought up. But there are other alternatives. I suggest 100-zero in the case of oil; that is, 100 per cent control on the part of the country in which the oil is located and zero per cent control on the part of the foreign oil company going in there. The investment can be protected by long-term contracts, stipulating repayment in a certain length of time. The operation of the project—getting the oil, refining it, and shipping it—can also be handled on a long-term contract.

The Mexican setup approaches what I have in mind. Mexico, after all, took over the actual ownership of the oil lands there, but they are operated through foreign capital on contract. I might suggest that ownership is just a long-term contract anyway. Without that contract, even 90 per cent or 100 per cent ownership is no protection.

With such enlightened policies about things like investment, we have reason to be encouraged. In the short run the Communists are able to exploit hunger and poverty by promising people the moon, and they do it extremely effectively. By the same token, however, this has begun to happen in many parts of the world (Burma and China are obvious examples): the Communists are simply unable to deliver the goods.

One reason for this is that they never begin by building their programs (as we see done in the Bell Report) on a broad outline dealing with food and sanitation as well as industry and hydroelectric development. Rather they focus on war protection, and the result of applying that kind of a five-year plan is not to give the common man the things he needs but to take things away from him.

We are at that point when our ideas and the way we put them over in the rest of the world are all-important. We can fight effectively with attitudes and with deeds—never forgetting plows, of course.

It seems to me that the summary of all this is contained in two phrases: (1) live with the people, (2) take a technician with you to emphasize the importance of constructive activity.

THE RED MENACE IN ASIA

Cornelio Balmaceda

The region comprising what is geographically known as Asia and the Far East is inhabited by nearly 1.1 billion people or more than half of the population of the world. However, it produces less than one-third of the world's food, and its share of the world's total income is only about one-fifth. Although well endowed with varied natural resources, this region remains underdeveloped; for many decades most of its millions of inhabitants have led a subhuman existence, and as a matter of fact their standards of living have been the lowest in the world.

The second World War brought about a chain of difficulties to the peoples of Asia and the Far East. Badly battered during the three and a half years of the Pacific war, the countries of this region suffered untold miseries as a direct result of the devastation and enormous destruction of lives and properties, the paralyzation of trade, and the collapse of their basic industries.

Recovery from this extensive war damage was slow and was rendered more and more difficult as new problems set in during the period of postwar readjustment. To the problems of reconstruction, underproduction, unemployment, inflation, and other economic difficulties were added social and political unrest, with all the concomitant problems.

The most serious problems, however, have been the spread of disturbances to peace and order, led by Communist agitators, and the deteriorating international situation. Less than five years after V–J day, war again broke out in Korea as the Communists from the North invaded the Republic of South Korea; and today, as you are fully aware, the Communist hordes of Red-dominated China are still locked in a prolonged war of attrition with the forces of the

NOTE: Mr. Balmaceda is Secretary of Commerce and Industry, Republic of the Philippines.

democratic nations under the leadership of the United States of America.

It is this same Communist agitation that is behind most, if not all, of the political and social troubles now taking place in many parts of Asia. In Indochina a bitter civil war is being fought between the Communist and anti-Communist elements in that country, while in practically all the other Asian countries Communists are working surreptitiously to overthrow the established governments.

It is evident that the Communists are bent on pursuing their objective of dominating the entire Asian continent as a part of their long-range scheme of world conquest. Their present activities in Asia would lend force to the popular belief that Soviet Russia is trying to get all of Asia into its orbit first in order to avoid having to fight on two fronts. But whether it is Asia first or not, it is clear that the menace is spreading and world-wide.

As it now exists in Asia, this menace is threatening to engulf the entire eastern continent and the countries of southeast Asia. It is a serious threat to the aspirations of half the human race who are struggling to achieve a higher standard of progress, human dignity, and a better way of life. It is fatal to the cause of democracy, which is just beginning to gain a wider and stronger foothold in that part of the world.

If we analyze the causes that have helped the spread of Communism in Asia, we shall meet the following conditions: (a) susceptibility of the Asian masses to new, revolutionary doctrines because of their age-old state of poverty and misery; (b) the devastation caused by the last war, which wrecked the economies of many Asian countries and caused more difficulties to the peoples and their governments; (c) resurgence of the spirit of nationalism; (d) lawlessness and moral decadence as a direct result of the war; and (e) geographical position of Asia relative to Soviet Russia.

One prevalent condition in Asia that we cannot overlook is the rampant poverty and misery among its millions of people. The Communists are taking advantage of this in propagating their doctrines. They find the poor, illiterate masses ready to give a willing ear to their Communist teachings as a possible remedy for their ills.

This condition was well presented in our recent session of the United Nations Economic Commission for Asia and the Far East that was held in central Asia last February, when the Prime Minister of Pakistan spoke before the Commission and said:

> The region which the Economic Commission for Asia and the Far East seeks to serve has suffered for many long decades from hunger and disease and here millions of people lead subhuman existence verging on a perennial state of almost-famine. Their lives have been one long tale of misery, unrelieved even by hope. Stricken by famines and epidemics, bowed down with care, they must often wonder why Destiny had made it so hard for them to live, when in other countries life was so different —so full of zest, so full of joy! At times like the present, when a large mass of humanity is in mental revolt against the conditions of life under which they were born, and which conditions give little promise of a change, when skepticism prevails and when the hearts of men rebel against the injustice of their hard destiny, people become easily responsive to any perverse teaching which offers an easy panacea for their ills. Their ignorance and illiteracy prevent an objective analysis of new ways of life offered to them. Their desperation makes them accept any hazardous path of life, if it only promises relief from their suffering. We must understand and take note of this state of mind if we are to save those peoples from unnecessary hazards, which may promise but never achieve a better way of life and a higher standard of living.

Posing as champions of the interests of the common man and advocates of social reforms, the agents of Communism work on the minds of the ignorant masses drugging them with sugar-coated promises of a new dispensation that, according to them, would improve their standard of living and remove all forms of social inequalities. Their doctrines often find fertile soil in the minds of those poor illiterate people who, because of their misery and abject poverty, easily fall for such enticing and alluring talks.

Another prevalent situation in Asia which Communism has thoroughly exploited in its efforts to gain support is the economic prostration that many Asian countries have suffered as a result of the last war. Economic dislocation, with all its attendant problems and difficulties, has given opportunities to the Communists to use their familiar systems of sabotage, sow confusion and chaos, and interfere with the execution of national programs of rehabilitation and recovery. They find that the longer the economic sufferings and difficulties of the people remain, the easier it is for them to achieve their ends.

After the war the nationalistic upheavals in different Asian countries that had long remained under alien domination gained in intensity as these countries saw the opportunity to throw off the shackles of colonialism. This situation has again been availed of by the Communists—stirring up hatred against the colonial powers and presenting them to the masses as "imperialists" and "exploiters."

Still another situation that favored the Communists was the rise of lawlessness and moral decadence among former war elements who have continued in possession of their weapons and have hied to the hills and joined the Communist ranks.

The other factor that has aided the Communist advance in Asia is the position of the Russian domain adjacent to the Asian continent. As early as 1921 the Sovietization of Outer Mongolia had begun, and it ended with the setting up of a Soviet republic in Mongolia which became Russia's strategic position for the advance into China. Less than twenty years later, taking advantage of the social and economic upheavals that swept China and capitalizing on the mistakes and corruption in the party that was then in power and the serious economic situation in that country after the last war, the Chinese Communists finally succeeded in overthrowing the Nationalist regime.

A usual Communist tactic is the Machiavellian practice of "divide and rule." After gaining the support of certain elements of the population in a country, by exploiting their political grudges or their ignorance and fanaticism, they incite them to use violence against the duly constituted authorities or the populace, which soon leads to local disorders or civil wars. Thus local groups are set against their own nationals and become tools and agents of their Communist mentors.

It was in this way that the Chinese Communists were set against the Kuomintang, and that the North Koreans were induced to cross the border and invade the South Koreans. It is in this way that the Vietnamese under Ho Chih Minh, the leader of the Communists in

Vietnam, are now up in arms against the government forces under Bao Dai; and it is in this way that local Communists and dissident elements are now fighting their own countrymen and committing atrocities in the Philippines, Burma, Indonesia, Malaya, India, and Pakistan.

Among the countries in Asia, the Philippines was the first to gain her complete independence after the last war. The new republic was proclaimed on July 4, 1946, as the culmination of the series of progressive steps that the United States had taken to bring us to our complete independence.

In the relations of Western nations with weaker nations in Asia, no country has been more sympathetic toward the national aspirations of an alien people than the United States has been toward the Philippines. A product of fifty years' training in the democratic system under the guidance of America, this young republic is now the far-flung bastion of democracy in Asia.

Independence came to the Philippines just as she was recovering from the devastations of war. More than three years of Japanese occupation had rendered her economy almost totally prostrate. At the end of the war her agricultural production was at its lowest. Industrial activity was at a standstill. Export industries were paralyzed, while normal trade was nil as a result of three years' suspension of commercial intercourse with the outside world. The young republic had literally to start from scratch to recuperate from the damages caused by the war and at the same time meet the added burdens and responsibilities incident to political freedom.

True to their usual pattern, the Communists in the Philippines took advantage of this very precarious situation in the country to revive their campaign and started aggressively to win more followers by capitalizing on the difficulties of the moment, poisoning the minds of the people against their own government, blaming it for all the economic ills that existed, emphasizing corruption and graft, and attacking the administration at every chance.

Before the war Communists in the Philippines were few and did not constitute even a remote threat to internal security. The backbone of the incipient Red movement was even believed broken when in the early 1930's their most outspoken leaders were charged with sedition and illegal association and subsequently convicted. The government was so firm in its belief that the movement had been nipped in the bud that the late President Quezon in 1937 pardoned and set free the convicted Communist leaders. President Quezon must not have foreseen at that time that a war was coming and that the evils concomitant to that war would be used to full advantage by these agents of the Kremlin to advance their cause and bring about the establishment of a Moscow-patterned society in the Philippines.

When the war against Japan was still in progress in the Philippines, a guerilla unit called "Hukbo ng Bayan Laban sa Hapon" or "Huks" was formed to fight the Japanese. Its leader, Luis Taruc, was a disciple of one of the prewar founders of the Philippine Communist party. People in Central Luzon gladly joined the organization as they would have joined any of the underground forces that operated against the Japanese. Many of them perhaps never thought that after the war they would be utilized by their superior officers for another fight—that they would be pitted against their own fellow countrymen and their strength used to destroy the democratic structure of the government.

After the cessation of hostilities these Huks did not disband. Instead they kept their organization in preparation for the subversive activities that they had already planned in conjunction with the world-wide Communist movement. They soon organized the armed force of the Communist Party of the Philippines, called the "Hukbong Mapagpalaya ng Bayan" or "People's Liberation Army." With this, they started their terroristic campaign, committing atrocities against officers of the law and innocent civilians.

As examples of Huk terrorist activities and armed aggression, the following wanton acts of murder, spoilage, arson, and destruction of private and public property, taken from actual cases recorded in public documents, may be cited:

(1) Raid on the municipal town hall of Majayjay, Laguna, on August 6, 1946, by an armed band of Huks. Police rifles, carbines, and pistols were carted away by the dissidents.

(2) On April 10, 1947, an army detachment while on its way to investigate a holdup in the barrio of San Miguel na Munti, Talavera, Nueva Ecija, was treacherously ambushed and fired upon by a band of Huks, killing the lieutenant and one private and wounding six others.

(3) In June, 1946, the town of Pantabangan, Nueva Ecija, was raided by an armed band of 180 Huks under the notorious character Alejandro Viernes, alias Stalin, who captured the town hall and raised the Huk flag for twenty-four hours. They demanded from the terror-stricken townspeople foodstuffs, such as rice, chickens, goats, and carabaos before leaving the town.

(4) One of the most dastardly acts of the Huks which stirred public indignation was the treacherous attack upon Mrs. Aurora A. Quezon, widow of the late President Manuel Quezon, and her party, on April 28, 1949, in Bongabong, Nueva Ecija. The party was ambushed by an undetermined number of Huks, and Mrs. Quezon, her daughter Baby Quezon, her son-in-law Philip Buencamino III, Mayor Ponciano Bernardo of Quezon City, Majors P. San Agustin and A. San Agustin, Lieutenant Lasam, and several enlisted men were mercilessly killed.

(5) On August 25, 1950, the army hospital in Camp Makabulos, Tarlac, was raided and set afire by the dissidents. Helpless patients lying in a hospital were killed, and a number of officers, enlisted men, and a Red Cross nurse were burned to death.

There can be no better proof of the relentless and ruthless activities of the Communists in the Philippines than the cases just mentioned as revealed in the "politburo" case recently tried in a Philippine court. This litany of atrocities perpetrated by the Huks is part of a general plan to gain control of the government by force of arms.

During the past two or three years the unbridled Communist propaganda appeared indeed to create a threatening situation. The sinister attempt of the Reds to weaken the national fabric seemed to be forging ahead. But after the government had reorganized its armed forces and a new Secretary of National Defense, Ramon Magsaysay, was appointed by the President of the Philippines, the offensive against the Huks began. Secretary Magsaysay led his fighting men into the mountains to rout the dissidents out of their hiding places. Then, last October 1950, the brains of the Communists were finally apprehended. Twenty-six Communist leaders were arrested and tried; and the court, after giving them a fair trial, convicted many of them of the complex crime of rebellion with murder and arson. Six were sentenced to death and others to life imprisonment and lighter prison terms. More than seven thousand documents seized from those arrested revealed in detail the Communists' plans. From these it was discovered that an all-out revolution led by the Communists was to have started last November 1950. The court found also that the leaders of the Communist Party had planned to hand the country over to Soviet Russia.

As a result of the government offensive the incipient revolution collapsed, and today the fear of a Communist-inspired revolution in the Philippines has faded, and its most outspoken leaders are now safely lodged behind bars.

This does not mean, however, that the menace of Communism in the Philippines has disappeared. It still exists and will continue to exist as long as the Communist organization there is not completely wiped out and the conditions upon which it feeds are not wholly changed. It will continue to exist as long as the Comintern can continue to threaten the peace of the free world.

The Communist Party in the Philippines has a very elaborate organization. On top is its national congress, and under it the central committee, politburo, organizational bureau, and the national courier (or communications) division, with couriers including women and young girls carrying messages. The national congress is the highest authority in the Communist Party. It guides and controls the whole party, formulates policies, and renders decisions on all political problems, tactics, and organizations. The military affairs are handled by a military committee, the secretariat, and the politburo. Besides these, there is a special warfare division which takes charge of the technological warfare against the enemy, such as the use of home-made bombs, "Molotov cocktails," land mines, booby traps, and so on. The armed force composed of Huks executes the orders from the top echelons of the party. The Huks also have an indoctrination school system, which they call Stalin University, scattered in the Huk-infested mountain areas.

The situation demanded the application of both military and economic measures by the Philippine Government. Among the government measures adopted are:

(1) Intensification of counterintelligence work by the Department of National Defense.

(2) Reinforcement of the armed forces.

(3) Strengthening of the economic structure of the country by adopting and implementing a nationwide economic mobilization program.

(4) Intensification of the food production campaign in order to raise much needed foodstuffs.

(5) Increasing the production of exportable products.

(6) Elimination of graft and corruption in the government service. An Integrity Board was especially created to investigate cases involving dishonesty and graft among the government personnel in an effort to cleanse the public service and restore the people's confidence in the government.

(7) Educating the masses on the true aims and practices of Communism through the radio and the printed word. The Philippine Information Council was organized by the government to spearhead the campaign of information against Communism.

(8) Development of the Kapatagan Valley settlement project in Mindanao for the future home of surrendered Huks and their families. Already about a hundred families of former Huks have been sent to the valley where they were given lands to cultivate in addition to farm tools and seeds to enable them to start a new life.

In order to carry these measures into effect, the government of the Philippines was compelled to divert a great part of its revenues to the expenses of our armed forces for internal security, with the result that nearly half of our annual government budget now goes to the maintenance of our Department of National Defense.

When it is considered that the needs of other public services, especially the public schools, had also increased as a result of the rise in our population, and also that government revenues had been greatly reduced because of the tremendous damage caused by the war to the normal productive activities, the deterioration of the financial situation of the government became inevitable. Government incomes could no longer meet the necessary expenditures, and when the government also undertook to carry out its economic reconstruction and development program, budget deficits had to be incurred.

Outside assistance, therefore, was necessary. Realizing fully the desperate situation immediately after the war, and living up to her plighted word to compensate for the extensive damage that had been wrought, the United States first gave war-damage payments. To make these payments, the United States Congress authorized an appropriation of four hundred million dollars besides one hundred and twenty million dollars for the repair and reconstruction of public roads, port facilities, and public health services, and the turning over to the Philippine government of war surplus property.

These measures helped to alleviate conditions in the first years of independence, but they were far from sufficient to repair all the war damage actually suffered and to enable the new government to meet the heavy requirements of the economic and peace-and-order situation.

In order to give the American people a complete report based on firsthand information, President Quirino requested President Truman to send an Economic Survey Mission to the Philippines. In sending the mission, President Truman said that it was "a symbol of the half century of intimate relationship between the Philippine and American peoples," and that it "will further solidify this historic association."

The mission, headed by General Edward W. Bell, did an excellent job, and, following its exhaustive survey and in line with its recommendations, more aid will be given through the United States Economic Cooperation Administration. The ECA program has just started, bringing a most timely stimulus to the recent pick-up in the general business situation in the Philippines. The business situation there today is definitely better now than one year or two years ago.

As President Quirino recently stated, the Philippines are now on the threshold of a new era. We have bridged the most crucial months with the help of the United States. The rising inflation has been checked; the foreign trade now shows a favorable balance, as exports continue to increase in volume and prices in this (United States) market remain high and attractive to producers.

We have begun to relax our system of controls, and we have even decontrolled many essential imports. As a result, a bigger flow of American goods to fill these imports is entering again. These have influenced domestic prices of essential goods to come down, and the consuming masses are beginning to feel the effects of a decreasing cost of living. These are indeed wholesome improvements which, if continued and maintained, will make us much stronger in our offensive against the enemies of our democratic government.

We cannot ignore the fact that democracy has its biggest stake in all Asia in the new Republic of the Philippines. That country has been called "the show window of democracy in the East." Its course, its fate, is being watched by the other countries in Asia, especially since the Philippines were set up as an independent republic by the greatest democratic nation in the world, and have had the longest contact with, and experience in the democratic system.

From this, it can be inferred that if the Philippines should fail, it will be a severe blow to democracy in Asia. If the Philippines should fail, America's work of fifty years in the Philippines will have failed.

In their desire to destroy the strong ties of friendship that bind the Philippines and the United States, the Communists in the Philippines have been resorting to the most dastardly and insidious means. Only a few months ago, the Communist Huks brought their bloody terrorism to the homes of Americans living in isolated places. An American couple running a dairy farm in the country some thirty miles from Manila were mercilessly murdered by a Communist band. Not long after, a mining camp owned and run by Americans was attacked by another band of Huks, but they were repelled before they had caused much damage.

Rumors then began to spread that the lives of American residents in the Philippines were in danger. But sensible people knew it was just another of the well-known Communist tactics of creating disorder and terrorism. Their real objective in this series of attempts against Americans was to stir up American feeling against the Philippines and Filipinos so that the aid and coöperation we are getting from America, which is proving so fatal to the cause of Communism in the country, would stop. Had these and similar incidents succeeded in creating a breach in American-Filipino relations, then we would have fallen into the Communist trap.

We can and surely shall save that young democracy from the encroachments of totalitarianism with the continued coöperation of our government and people with the government and people of the United States. We must realize, however, that time is of the essence. We cannot delay taking the adequate measures that the exigencies of the situation demand. These measures need not be too costly or risky to the lives of our men. On the contrary, the measures can be both peaceful and constructive.

One of the most effective measures adopted in the Philippines is that of giving lands to dissident Communists who have surrendered to the government and who have pledged to return to the realm of lawful and peaceful living. These surrendered Huks have confessed that they were deceived by the Communists who promised to give them lands that they might own and cultivate.

The campaigns waged by the Communists among the peasants in Central Luzon encouraged the belief that the underlying cause of Communism there was the agrarian situation. The truth, however, is that the peasants were misled by the Communist teachings of "dictatorship of the proletariat" and the promise of complete elimination of all social classes, which would give them a chance to own most of what now belongs to the rich. The opportunity to own lands and to become an independent farmer able to support a family holds a strong appeal to the poor people, especially to those who have long been living as tenants. If the offer comes to one, he is prone to accept it, even if it is from a Communist.

In the Philippines, there are wide tracts of agricultural lands in many parts of the archipelago still untilled. Our country now has a population of twenty million, but with its unused areas the land can easily support a population of eighty million. The Army of the Philippines and the government itself have begun opening many of these idle but rich agricultural lands for settlement by the landless inhabitants, including the hitherto misguided elements who have now abandoned the Communists.

Hundreds of poor families have already become new settlers. Our government's policy of giving land to the landless so that they can work and live as peaceful citizens is yielding excellent results. One of the new settlements is exclusively for surrendered former Communists who are now happier and wiser, living with contentment in their new homes. They are new but firm believers in the free and democratic way of life.

Here, therefore, is a bloodless, peaceful, constructive, and most effective way to fight Communism. The effects of the system do not end with the individual ex-Communists themselves, for they induce many others of their former ilk to abandon Communism.

The only limitation to this policy is the insufficiency of funds to finance each settlement project. Money must be provided to enable the new settlers to start, clear the new land, buy their work animals and implements, build their shelters, buy their seeds and plant. We cannot simply place them in the wild forest or idle land and then abandon them to their fate, for then they would be entirely helpless, they would suffer more, and we should only make them more bitter against life and society.

This is the difficulty that the Philippine Government is meeting in financing this new system of combatting Communism. As we have seen, its funds are very limited compared with the requirements of the many essential things it has to provide for, especially the maintenance of the army for internal security.

We should like to recommend this peaceful way of combatting Communism to the other countries in Asia, where new lands are still available for acquisition by Communists who surrender and show a real desire to abandon Communism. We should commend the same peaceful way to governments and peoples in the democracies who have the means to give financial assistance not only to those within their respective countries but also to other needy democratic countries that are now facing the threat of Communism.

The Philippines are hopeful of securing from America more liberal financial aid for carrying out this anti-Communist policy on a wider scale than is possible with the very limited funds of our government. The money we can put into this project will be much less than the amount we have been spending or are willing to spend to finance an actual war. Why should we be so much more ready to pour money into the financing of wars after they have broken out than to spend money in order effectively to prevent the wars?

It is indeed heartening to read the message sent by President Truman to the United States Congress, in which he has asked for eight and a half billion dollars for a new foreign aid program "to help thwart Communist dreams of world conquest" and "to strengthen the defenses of free nations around the world." This is a part of President Truman's Point Four program which has brought a new hope to underdeveloped nations.

In his recent message, President Truman specifically mentioned that the underdeveloped countries in Asia produce strategic materials "which are essential to the defense and economic health of the free world" and that "production of these materials must be increased." The President added:

> "The development of the resources of these countries helps them by raising their standard of living and increasing their resistance to communist subversion and helps the whole free world in increasing their supply of raw materials essential to defense and to an expanding world economy."

Coming back now to the general situation in Asia, the defense of democracy from the onslaughts of totalitarianism in that part of the world requires definite and practical measures on the part of the democratic nations. Such measures should include:

(1) The amelioration of the lot of the landless populations in countries where new lands are still available for settlement.

(2) Acceptance of the reality of a new force in the life and history of Asian nations, realizing for them their rights of national freedom, human dignity, and mutual respect in their relations with the other nations of the world.

(3) A system of economic and financial assistance with a much broader scope than the Marshall Plan in order to meet the urgent requirements of both their reconstruction and their development.

(4) A system of mutual coöperation that will assure to the free countries of Asia the same benefits of joint action for the defense of democracy in the East that the Atlantic Pact gives to the nations of Western Europe.

(5) A vigorous educational and information drive in Asia to save the poor and illiterate masses from falling an easy prey to Communistic propaganda, to unmask the myth of Communism, and to demonstrate the true blessings of democracy and freedom.

Some ill feelings and old grudges nurtured by many long years of subjugation by old colonial powers are still strong irritants in the relations between newly liberated nations in Asia and their former sovereign powers. The Red propagandists are quick to play upon these irritants in order to serve their own purposes. The new force of nationalism in these countries should therefore be considered in orienting the policy of Western powers toward their former subjects lest a wedge be created which the enemies of democracy would be only too quick to use to their own advantage.

If the present conditions of backwardness, misery, hunger, and disease upon which Communistic propaganda thrives so well in the East are to be removed, the more advanced and prosperous nations, especially the United States, must extend greater economic and financial aid to these underdeveloped countries.

What Asia needs in this respect is more than a Marshall Plan. The task to be accomplished is not just the restoration of the devastated economies to their prewar conditions, as in Europe. That would not be enough. Asia needs development. Its dormant resources must be developed and utilized to afford the necessary income to the hundreds of millions of peoples in Asia in order to enable them to raise their standards of living. More efficient and scientific methods of agriculture must be introduced to replace the antiquated and inefficient farming methods that are still in use. Industrialization, "know-how," and modern technology must be used to raise their standard of economic development, intensify their production, and provide more sources of income and employment, especially in those countries and places where agriculture can no longer adequately support the size of the populations.

To be able to implement their industrialization programs, these countries need equipment, machinery, and materials from the West. The Western nations must help them in order to give them the necessary material means to strengthen the defense of democracy in Asia.

Let me invite the attention of businessmen to the great opportunities for investment and the employment of technical knowledge and skill in new commercial and business enterprises in Asia and the Far East. The new trend in the expansion of world commerce is clearly toward Asia and the Pacific Area. This is only natural after the development, perhaps to the fullest extent now, of the countries of Europe and North America and the entire Atlantic Area.

The century which preceded the outbreak of the first World War in 1914 witnessed a tremendous advance in science and industry in Europe—an advance which made that part of the world the busiest center of international commerce. During the two world wars, the United States of America was called upon to supply most of the needs of the world and had to expand her industries and trade far beyond the requirements of her own domestic market. The United States thus became the real arsenal of the world and the greatest industrial nation and center of world commerce.

After the reconversion and reconstruction period following the second World War, industry and commerce had to find new fields for expansion. The surplus capital and technical knowledge of the highly developed nations must be kept employed and on the lookout for green pastures to develop.

In this respect Asia, because of the vast extent of her undeveloped resources and her vast potential market, comprising more than half of the human race whose standards of living and purchasing power are still very low, is undoubtedly the "promised land" of the future. Economic development in this region heretofore has been largely confined to the partial exploitation of the agricultural areas and the production of raw materials for export to the industrial countries. Industrial development is almost untapped, except within a limited area in the north.

In thinking ahead for business, the businessmen of America must not fail to explore the business opportunities awaiting them in Asia.

It is indeed deplorable that the menace of totalitarian aggression should now stand in the way of that development. If we remove that menace, we shall surely see the tide of investments and developments sweeping over Asia.

Despite this menace, however, I can tell you that there are many businessmen of America who are strong of faith and strong of heart and will, and who are even now starting and building up new business enterprises and making new investments in the Philippines and in other parts of Asia and the Far East, undeterred by the danger of Communistic aggression. These businessmen have faith in the future. They have confidence in the ability of the forces of democracy to stem the threatening tide of Soviet imperialism.

About the middle of last year, and shortly after the signing of the North Atlantic Pact, President Elpidio Quirino of the Republic of the Philippines conceived the plan of forming a Southeast Asia Union. In explaining his plan President Quirino said:

"Last April, following the initialing of the North Atlantic Pact in Paris, I declared on behalf of our Government that it was imperative that the free countries of Southeast Asia, with the active support of the United States, should consider at the earliest possible moment the conclusion of a parallel safeguard for Asia.

Today, the need of pursuing this line of thought is pressing and urgent. It was and still is necessary for the Asian countries to consult and to coöperate with one another in order to hasten their emergence as independent countries. But the great danger that confronts us at this moment is the tide of totalitarian subversion and conquest which threatens to engulf the very freedom we have won or others expect to win. This menace is on the ascendant, and in order to meet it we must forge stronger bonds than exist at present.

It was because of this imminent danger that I conceived in the Baguio conversations last month the necessity of accelerating the process of establishing a Union, predicated upon the independence and sovereignty of the peoples of Southeast Asia and the countries bordering the Pacific so that, masters of their own destiny, they can concentrate their attention to their coördinated full development in order to ensure their stability and security and thus contribute to world peace and advancement. I envisaged such a union to be essentially an act of common faith on the economic, political and cultural level, in tune with the work of the ECAFE and the program of the UNESCO and that it would involve no military commitments. For I am convinced that in the long run our strongest defense against totalitarian subversion would lie in providing a life of substance and contentment and promoting higher living standards among the Asian peoples. Thus it would be a real union on the basis of common counsel and assistance for the preservation of peace, democracy, and freedom in Asia."

This plan has lately been gaining support among the democratic countries both in and outside southeast Asia. The beginnings that have been made in forming such a union among Asian countries should be pursued toward their early realization in order to pool together the strength of the free nations in Asia in the defense of democracy.

Lastly, the organized and ceaseless propaganda by the Communists must be met with an effective counterpropaganda on the side of democracy. This is particularly necessary in Asia and the Far East. There should be a wide dissemination of true information on the doings and practices of the Soviets. The people should be properly informed as to what Communism really stands for and what it does to those who fall into its trap. They should be told of the tenets of Communism—its denial of the existence of God, of the right of a human being to choose the kind of occupation that he thinks best and to enjoy the fruits of his own toil; and its denial also of the basic human freedoms—freedom of worship, freedom of speech and of the press, and freedom of assembly. Then they cannot be blindly misled by any kind of propaganda that may be pressed on them.

At the same time, we have to keep our own people in the free nations strong and firm in their faith in democracy. They should have a clear concept of its real meaning, its benefits, and its practices. They should understand well the meaning of freedom as opposed to totalitarianism. We have to disseminate correct and true information which is needed to guide the thinking of men and women everywhere in the present struggle between the two opposing ideologies. If, as someone has rightly said, wars are born in the minds of men, then it is our supreme duty as citizens of the free world to build the defenses of peace in the minds of men.

AN ECONOMIC PROGRAM FOR ASIA

Raymond W. Miller and C. Leigh Stevens

During the past four years, 250,000 inhabitants of free Asia per day have gone under the materialistic, imperialistic rule of the Soviets. The majority of them, in my opinion, have gone voluntarily. Yes, they have been deluded, preached to, fed a lot of falsehoods; but nevertheless they have been seduced voluntarily, very largely because the rest of the world failed to recognize that the problem of the Asian farmer was its problem.

Even if we disregard the humanitarian impulse, purely selfish reasoning tells us that we cannot afford to lose the countries of Asia as friends, rich as they are in many resources which we either lack completely or have not in sufficient quantity. Especially can we not afford to lose them when doing so means that our loss will be the Communists' gain.

Today, then, these problems abroad are our problems. The farmers of Asia are questioning; they are wondering why they should always live in dirt and in disease and in despair. And if we cannot convince them that we have the answers to their problems, the Communists, who are notorious for taking advantage of such opportunities, can.

Let us examine this rebellious Far Eastern farmer and see how he lives, for only by understanding the problems he is facing can we make even the initial step toward solving them. This man is born into debt, lives in debt, and passes on a heritage of debt to his children. One of the chief reasons for this situation is the land-tenancy system.

NOTE: Mr. Miller is Consultant to the Food and Agriculture Organization, United Nations, and Visiting Lecturer, Harvard Business School; Mr. Stevens is Special Advisor to Director General, Food and Agriculture Organization, United Nations, and Visiting Lecturer, Harvard Business School.

The observations of the two authors have been combined.

The Asian has a small plot of land ranging from three to five acres. Here, he and his wife work barefooted ten, twelve, even fifteen hours a day. When he finally does reap his meager harvest, he has to pay not 20 per cent or even 30 per cent but in many cases 70 per cent of this harvest for rent. It is situations like this that bring despair. Because of the oppressive rents charged by the landlords, the farmer will often find it not worth his while to get a better-than-average harvest, for the whole of the increase (or even more) may be taken from him in increased rents.

Land reform should be a common denominator in every program for adjustment to modern conditions in underdeveloped areas. And land reform can be accomplished. We proved that in Japan where the successful land-reform program of MacArthur's administration has created a large land-owning class which is a strong and natural bulwark against the Soviets. We proved it also in South Korea where very beneficial rights of ownership are now enjoyed.

But that is not all. In many of these places, even where reform has been accomplished, the farms are so small (ranging from two to five acres) that *voluntary* association into coöperatives also is necessary. In all cases where coöperatives have been given a fair test, they have proved that they can serve as pace setters toward a better rural life, if honestly and efficiently operated in the public interest. They should be organized on a nonprofit basis, acting as purchasing or marketing agents for the producer. Buying as an individual, the small farmer would find it very difficult to afford the fertilizer for his crop or an improved farm implement. That is why the coöperative is a necessary follow-up to land reform.

Land hunger is not the only kind in Asia. These people do not have enough to eat or wear or a decent shelter over their heads. Their resulting weakness makes them very susceptible to disease; indeed, villages where a third of the people are ill with malaria are not uncommon. Such conditions arise from the fact that the *known* methods of conservation of natural resources and of increasing, distributing, and utilizing products from farms, forests, seas, and mines have not been made available. This could be remedied through use of the techniques of extension wherein "know-how" can be taken from where it is to where it is needed, and made useful and understandable through "show-how."

But we have to face the fact that mechanization is *not* a cure-all in Asia. It is impractical for several reasons:

(1) The farmer distrusts any radical innovations; he resents the "foreigner" trying to change his way of life.

(2) Besides being unwilling, he is unable to use or care for the machines properly.

(3) Asia lacks "sources of power" with which to run such machinery. Oil and gasoline are scarce; roads, when available, are primitive; assuming that hydroelectric power sources exist, there are no transmission lines or generating plants. Moreover, supplying trained man power and spare machine parts as well as servicing machinery would be almost impossible.

(4) The periods between rain and drought when machines such as tractors could be run are generally very short. What these people need is a large animal force that can go to work right after the rainy season.

We have attempted to convince the educated people in the Far East of the desirability of mechanizing Eastern agriculture. We ship tractors all over the place. We ship rice combines to India, half as big as the fields they are supposed to operate in, and this is the literal truth. We blissfully assume that we can support a mechanized agriculture in the Far East. We forget that American mechanization is not based upon the tractor; it is based upon the automobile, the pick-up truck, because without the proper repair part the tractor will not run.

And still we ship Cadillacs and tractors to the Far East at big prices. American industry never worries about sources of power. If we want a ten-thousand horsepower motor, somebody will build it for us. Out there the source of power is a pair of bullocks. It is going to be a pair of bullocks for a long time to come.

It would seem practical, not to mention the fact that it will be cheaper, therefore, to give those bullocks something to move. The iron in one tractor will make the metal part for about 4,000 plows, something the Asian farmer needs and is able to use. It would take less than one half of one per cent of our total annual steel production to provide such a tool for *every* farmer in India.

Much can be done in Asia by approaching problems at the grass-roots level. With some simple technical improvements in farm implements, for example, a tremendous increase in food production can be brought about. A few basic improvements over the traditional *desi* plow would allow the farmer to cultivate fifteen acres a year instead of the present average of five. Again, some simple improvements in the existing mechanism of the water wheels of India will enable the camel (or any other source of power used) to pump about four times as much water as at present.

Every dollar spent in teaching the Asians improved methods and techniques in meeting problems like those of fertilization, reforestation, animal husbandry, and crop rotation will accomplish as much as ten or more dollars spent on mechanization. These countries are not yet in that stage of development where a concentration on building up industry is in order. Agriculture must be built up first, and after an agricultural surplus has been achieved, then the abundance of labor, raw materials, and power resources can be combined with the known construction and manufacturing methods and chemurgic techniques to meet the need for industrial goods and services. But the potential man power for such industrial development must first be released; at present it is tied down because purchasing power is so low that most people have to grow their own food to get enough to eat.

Improving existing methods of agriculture, accordingly, should be the first move; then more food can be produced by less man power. It should again be emphasized that such improvements can be as simple and basic as replacing a long-handled hoe with a short-handled one.

An area where the means of transportation and communication are nonexistent might be compared to a body having no veins and arteries for the transmission of blood. Asia is such an area. The primitive state of transportation and communication systems there is another very serious deterrent to progress. Marketing and purchasing are necessarily conducted on a very localized scale (if at all);

rich sources of supply are not exploited for lack of incentive on the part of the surrounding villages. Technical "know-how," even when available, is so isolated that in many parts of Asia the maximum capacity of distribution of information is the round-trip distance one man can walk or row in one day.

Labor in abundance is available to build the roads and lay the rails. What is needed is technical assistance in engineering and surveying problems and perhaps a small (because of the cheapness of labor) financial investment. When the investment starts paying off, the money can be returned. Remember that Asia does not need superhighways or anything resembling them. All that is needed is a fairly hard road, wide enough for a wagon or two, and a pair of low-speed rails along the easiest way between two points.

Another problem that a little of our technical "know-how" can go a long way toward solving is that of nutrition. We have done a great deal of harm in this respect by the introduction of food-processing equipment which preserves the visual appeal of food but takes away a large percentage of the natural vitamins and minerals. Food is of little value if it is not made available to the digestive system in such a way that it can sustain normal physical life. In many of the major rice-producing areas, for example, hulling, milling, washing, and cooking are done in such a manner as to eliminate most of the minerals and vitamins before the rice is eaten. In many cases, Western processing methods are largely to blame. We know both the right way and the wrong way of processing foods, and we have taught them the wrong way.

Besides this, great quantities of rice and other primary foods are lost yearly through faulty and antiquated methods of storage. The rats consume the rice not only in the granaries but in the fields as well. At least 10 per cent of all the cereal harvested—or the amount of these foods moving in world trade—is destroyed by rats and other pests. Our methods of fighting rodents and insect pests could be made available to Asia, preferably by demonstration, at a minimum of cost. The result would mean a maximum of food saved.

Our policy for Asia should be one of showing the people how to help themselves. We could use local adaptations under native administration of the American county demonstration agent system, which made modern agriculture possible in this country. The development of extension service techniques, using scientifically trained nationals with an understanding of local cultures, traditions, and peculiar problems, would do wonders in a short time for underdeveloped areas. By lifting agriculture and fisheries even one small step up from the primitive stage, the extra amount of capital—both human and material—required to start many areas on the road to comprehensive economic development would be attained.

Diplomacy is not enough to reach the people of Asia, but the United States can work at the grass-roots level through organizations like the United Nation's Food and Agricultural Organization, our own Department of Agriculture's Office of Foreign Agricultural Relations, and the Technical Coöperation Administration in Charge of the Point Four Program.

The FAO, for example, works with the primary producers to help them attain not only enough to feed, clothe, and shelter themselves, but something extra which can be used to help the economy expand. There is much to be done in Asia, but it cannot be done with an air of condescension or superiority. These people are as proud and as resentful of being talked down to as we would be.

The American businessman—the man who helps form the policies of American industry—should take an interest in the problems of Asia. He should make dead certain that the things he sells abroad are things that are good for the area. Of course, he should allow himself a profit—business has to have a profit to continue—but he should never lose a sense of responsibility. Our idea of good business practice, of constantly trying to put ourselves in the other fellow's shoes, of trying to look at problems and proposals from the point of view of all concerned, applies with a special force to the matter of our relations with other parts of the world. We should attempt to help people build on what *they* have rather than on what *we* have: There is more grain cut in Asia with an eight-inch sickle by boys and girls and men and women on their knees than is cut in the entire rest of the world with combine harvesters.

The people of Asia will realize their highest potentialities only if given the opportunity to work voluntarily with others and if there is an incentive in the form of a reasonable reward for their efforts. Central Asia with its materialistic despotic system of government is trying to take these people with them and tell them they are going to have a new life; Central Asia is succeeding too well. We can only retain these people by being good neighbors. The job ahead may be difficult, but the need for our making the effort is great.

THE ATLANTIC PACT NATIONS

Thomas D. Cabot

It would be more than rash for anyone to make predictions of what the next few years will bring in our relations with the countries in the North Atlantic area. I know of no crystal ball that will show American businessmen or American statesmen what the events of the future might be. But I think the economic and political and moral developments of the last five or ten years point to trends that are unmistakable and that may be used with reasonable confidence as guides for the future.

To appreciate the full impact of the changes that have taken place during the past ten years in the area of the Atlantic Pact, one has to think back to the days between the two world wars, when economic isolationism was more or less the rule and political coöperation was about as potent as the League of Nations. These twin forces of economic hostility and political isolationism worked behind tariff walls, import quotas, exchange controls, customs regulations, and a maze of artificial barriers to trade. They worked destructively to tie up the European economies and to tie up our own, with the result that we headed into a world-wide depression and eventually another world war. We in the United States were as guilty as everyone else in thinking that economic and political security could be built behind the cloistered walls of national boundaries.

With the harsh shock of the second World War, there developed a new climate of ideas, brought about by necessity and providing the forerunner of the new international concept which we are developing today. With the exigencies of the war all too clear, an unprecedented degree of coöperation grew up between the United States and its Allies across the Atlantic. The Lend-Lease program promoted a new moral unity among the Allies that fed further

NOTE: Mr. Cabot is Director of National Security Affairs, United States Department of State.

collaboration in other fields. That moral unity was crucial. It gave us a base on which to coöperate in meeting other crises in other places at other times. Once we had found a way of breaking through the moral or spiritual barrier, there was hope that we could break through the harder crust of economic barriers and political barriers.

The net result of our coöperative effort during the war was a new determination among the great majority of nations to work together to solve mutual problems after the war. The United Nations provided the vehicle through which this new determination could be effectively carried out. But within the North Atlantic area, the nations began to survey the age-old problems that had harassed them and undertook to carry the new spirit into new associations within their own area.

The Western European nations came out of the war devastated and on the verge of economic collapse. Despite the tremendous resources which we poured into our war effort, we came out of the struggle economically strong, with a larger and more efficient production capacity and more trained workers. With such capacity we were capable of assuming heavy responsibilities for the rehabilitation of other less fortunate areas without serious impact on our own standard of living.

In those first few years after the war the nations in the North Atlantic area faced one of the most critical tests of survival. To go back deliberately to the old pattern of economic and political hostility and isolationism was, on the face of it, impossible. But could we—all of us—break through the old pattern sufficiently to release ourselves from its shackles? Could we actually sit down and negotiate new economic agreements and political agreements and move hard cash across the table? That would be the criterion of success in abandoning the old pattern.

I would not hesitate to say that the concrete developments in the North Atlantic area since the war give us every reason to believe that we are well on the road to a new kind of relationship in which economic, political, and spiritual coöperation are the marked features.

The willingness of Americans to share the burden of European rehabilitation under the Marshall Plan, and indeed the interest and zest with which we entered into the job, and the public realization that it was in our mutual interest have proved to be some of the greatest motivations for closer coöperation among the European nations themselves. The Organization for European Economic Cooperation has been extremely important in getting across to the people of Western Europe the possibilities of joint effort and in planning a united attack on the problems of economics and finance which were common to all.

In these efforts the trend toward integration and coöperation in economic, political, and military matters is unmistakable. In 1947, Belgium, the Netherlands, and Luxembourg took the decision to form a customs union known as "Benelux." France and Italy are discussing similar arrangements.

Trade barriers are being broken down in other ways, too. There has been the General Agreement on Tariffs and Trade. Three international conferences have been held since the end of the second World War in which more and more countries are participating in negotiations to reduce trade restrictions. At Torquay, England, this year thirty-four nations, representing more than four-fifths of all world trade, negotiated agreements.

Perhaps the most dramatic effort of European nations to overcome economic separatism is contained in the Schuman Plan. A little over a year ago Foreign Minister Schuman of France inspired the free world with his government's proposal to merge the coal and steel industries of France and Germany, and any other European country that wished to participate, into a single market. Recently, six nations signed the treaty that will put the Schuman Plan into effect. They were Belgium, France, Western Germany, the Netherlands, Italy, and Luxembourg.

The Schuman Plan itself is a highly complex one. Its economic and administrative details testify to the maze of barriers that it will have to overcome. But over and above the interesting details, several overwhelmingly significant points stand out: first, six nations of Europe are willing, for the first time, to delegate powers of economic life and death to a supranational organization and have agreed to enforce the rulings of the organization with effective fines and sanctions. Second, the revitalizing factor of competition will be injected into an industry which has been marked for its lack of competition and the host of economic ills that have followed from this unhealthy condition. And third, the welding of new economic ties among nations which have been traditionally hostile augurs well for a new political relationship in which it will be to their mutual advantage to be peaceful and coöperative. An important part of the Schuman Plan is to build up production where it is most efficient with minimum regard for national boundaries.

The novelty of these developments cannot be overestimated. In the success of the Schuman Plan may well lie the future of Europe. If these nations can put the plan into smooth operation, can overcome the hardships that the plan will impose on certain people and certain nations at its inception, and can maintain the spirit of the agreement as well as the letter of it, the plan may serve as a pilot project for new political unity in Europe.

Suffice it to say that American statesmen and American businessmen will do well to watch this progress most carefully. It has great catalytic potentialities in shaping a European renaissance. Through the Schuman Plan we may be able to observe even more closely the effect of the new moral forces. It is obvious even now that economic coöperation in the North Atlantic area is both supported by and acts as a support for collective action in the political and military arena.

With national autarchy on the decline, regional organizations have sprung up. The Council of Europe is making initial efforts toward a European parliament, and since the adoption of the North Atlantic Treaty on April 4, 1949, important steps have been taken to build NATO—the North Atlantic Treaty Organization—into an association of free democratic nations which by political, military, and economic coöperation can create the collective security needed as a deterrent against the threat of aggression. It is through NATO, as you know, that the forces for the defense of the North Atlantic area are being built.

I should like to take a moment to talk about NATO and the program for rearmament of Europe. I believe they are important factors in the future for which businessmen must plan. Furthermore, the welding of twelve independent nations into a volunteer team for a common purpose, which is at once political, economic, and military, is an exercise in organization from which business might well derive a lesson.

Because each of the three purposes—political, military, and economic—is the responsibility of a different minister in most of the member governments, it is perhaps natural that NATO started as a complex of committees of ministers with indefinite functions and infrequent meetings. Now some simplification has emerged. The work formerly done by temporary international committees is now being handled by boards which are in permanent session. Also, some executive machinery has been established, of which the most important and dramatic example has been the creation of an integrated European military force under the command of General Eisenhower. General Eisenhower takes his direction from the Standing Group in Washington, an international military executive body comparable to the Combined Chiefs of Staff in the second World War. The Standing Group gets political guidance from the Council of Deputies in London, through which the twelve governments are in continuous consultation.

It is conceivable that Western Europe, given sufficient time, could rearm for its collective security without our help. But time is the key factor. The disastrous effects of the second World War imposed formidable economic obstacles to Western European rearmament. Meanwhile, the Soviet Union, by subjecting the peoples under its control to a slave economy, had obtained a long lead in military power. Under such circumstances, even the decision to make a start was a difficult one to reach; perhaps no free people, no democratic society, could be expected to summon the resolution to shoulder such a heavy and uncertain burden.

Realizing the vital importance to the United States of maintaining a viable, strong, free Europe, we have through the combined aid of our European Recovery Program and Mutual Defense Assistance Program given the impetus so that a good beginning has been made toward this objective. The Mutual Security Program now before our Congress proposes to continue the strengthening of the North Atlantic area—to use in the most effective way the great, but limited, economic strength of the United States to advance its own security and welfare.

This is a program to join our economic strength with that of other countries for the common good. It is an economy program in that the dollars we spend will build more strength in support of our own security than we could build at home with the same amount of money. Spending our funds to help Europe defend itself not only is a less expensive way for us to build our own defense; it is perhaps the only way of securing more than a bleak future spent trying to protect our own shores against constant threat from those who seek world domination.

When I say that our aid to Western Europe represents an economic bargain, I do not wish to imply that we are thinking in any way of sponsoring a mercenary military force, nor of asking the Europeans to undertake the major burden of defending the United States. Instead, our policy is based on the simple principle that if we help the Europeans to achieve the determination and the strength to defend themselves, the total strength of the free world will be greatly multiplied, and, as a direct result, the cost of maintaining our own defenses will be far less than it would otherwise be. Our aid program is a financial bargain in the same way that it is cheaper for a man to give a fire extinguisher to a next door neighbor whose house is in flames than it is for him to risk having the fire spread to his own house. Our program is neither cynical and calculating, on the one hand, nor starry-eyed and visionary, on the other; it is a matter of ordinary common sense.

Both here and abroad there are many earnest thinkers who believe that the political, military, and economic integration of the North Atlantic community should lead to some new superfederation of states. Public opinion may ultimately support such a goal. Personally, I take the optimistic view that with the economy of Western Europe rebuilt and its defense secured, and with a continuation of the trend toward political and moral unity, there will be no need of new formal relationships substantially more rigid than those of common membership and support of NATO and of the United Nations.

In any case, there is now general recognition of the multiple threats that face our society. I feel sure that the American people, and especially American business, will have the wisdom, the patience, and the firmness of purpose to use this new spirit of coöperation to lead the world to a better tomorrow.

MOBILIZATION OF OUR WESTERN ALLIES

N. E. Halaby, Colonel G. A. Lincoln, H. van Buren Cleveland, Ridgway B. Knight, and Frederick Cone

Introduction

It may be useful to begin by reviewing briefly some of the past events which have brought us to where we are now in our planning for peace through collective defensive strength.

The "Truman Doctrine" speech calling for aid to Greece and Turkey was made in May 1947. One month later, at the Harvard Commencement, General Marshall made his famous speech which led to the development of the Marshall Plan. In March 1948 the Brussels Treaty was signed by England, France, Belgium, the Netherlands, and Luxembourg, and in May 1948 that initiative was followed by the Vandenberg Resolution, out of which grew the North Atlantic Treaty. There were negotiations on this treaty during the following winter and spring, and a climax, I think, was reached when the Norwegians decided against neutrality and in favor of the Western coalition. In the spring of 1949 we introduced the first Mutual Defense Assistance Program, and in April the North Atlantic Treaty was signed.

It will be recalled that during this time the Communist revolution in China had just about succeeded in denying a large part of Asia to the Western countries. In July 1949 the Senate endorsed the principle of collective security overwhelmingly in ratifying the North Atlantic Treaty by a vote of 82 to 13. Shortly thereafter we heard

NOTE: Mr. Halaby is Assistant to the Administrator for Internal Security Affairs, ECA; Colonel Lincoln is Professor of Social Science, Military Academy, West Point; Mr. Cleveland is Deputy Director, European Program Division, ECA; Mr. Knight is with the Office of European Regional Affairs, Department of State; and Mr. Cone is Economist, Office of Defense Mobilization.

The introduction and conclusion are drawn from Mr. Halaby's remarks; the military, economic, and political viewpoints represent the observations of Colonel Lincoln, Mr. Cleveland, and Mr. Knight, respectively; and the discussion of raw materials is by Mr. Cone.

that the Russians had staged an atomic explosion, and we realized slowly during the succeeding months the consequences of having lost our monopoly over atomic power.

In September 1949 the North Atlantic Treaty Organization was formed, and the Mutual Defense Assistance Program was approved by Congress. In January 1950, the chiefs of the twelve North Atlantic Treaty powers agreed on a strategic concept for the defense of the area. In the same month President Truman decided to build the H-Bomb.

Then in June of 1950 came the attack on the Republic of South Korea.

Since that time we have come a long way. The North Atlantic Treaty Organization has projected an integrated defense force, with a supreme commander in Western Europe. It has gone far toward agreement on German participation. In December 1950, shortly after he proclaimed a national emergency, the President appointed General Eisenhower to this command, and has since submitted a program of eight and a half billion dollars worth of military and economic aid for our Allies. The military forces necessary are now being raised, trained, and equipped so as to meet international defense plans.

This march of events has committed the United States to a policy that is as complex as it is important. Let us look now at some of its ramifications and implications.

Military Aspects

I must start by pointing out that nothing I say should be interpreted as the policy of the United States Government or of the Defense Department. But let me add, immediately, that any similarity between my views and the present broad policies of the United States with reference to security in the present danger is deliberate, planned, and intentional. I happen, as a private citizen and taxpayer, to believe that the current government policies in the field of discussion are our best guarantee of survival.

It seems to me that the most useful contribution I can make is to provide an outline of the more military aspects of our assistance to our Allies. In attempting such an outline, I am aware—as is everybody else—of the impossibility of effecting any clear separation of so-called military aspects from political aspects or economic aspects or, for that matter, psychological aspects.

Our subject implicitly accepts certain basic principles and estimates. I do not propose to question that there is in the world today a serious threat to the security of the United States.

It always alarms me when people misinterpret George Washington's Farewell Address, and particularly his advice about avoiding foreign entanglements. Washington stated that the United States was remote from Europe, and he proceeded from there without arguing the point. I would suggest that the United States right now is *not* remote from any place. Indeed, one of our greatest concerns is that we are not sufficiently remote from Russia or Russian bases, and that indeed sometime in the not too far distant future the Russians might be flying airplanes over us.

Furthermore, we are in an uncomfortable situation where the security threat of Western Europe is one and the same thing as the security threat of the United States, which was not true in George Washington's time. What he did say on the matter of security, as I recall, ran something like this: "Take care to maintain an adequate military posture." That clause has usually been forgotten through the decades by the isolationists. Also: "We can safely trust to temporary alliances under extraordinary circumstances." That is a sentence that always seems to show tremendous foresight on the part of George Washington; it is applicable to the present day. We now have extraordinary circumstances.

So I am going to proceed on the assumption that we accept the need for allies and accept the need for their mobilization in a mutual effort to meet the present security threat of the free world.

It is well to analyze what we mean by the word "allies." Aside from our very general commitments under the United Nations, we have specific alliances with two groups of nations—the Latin American countries under the Rio Pact and the north Atlantic countries through the North Atlantic Treaty. Referring back to the United

Nations, we are at the present time fighting side by side in Korea with forces from nations which are members of neither of these alliances—troops of Thailand, the Philippines, Turkey, and Greece, for example. Furthermore, we now propose in the Mutual Security Program to give economic and arms aid to countries such as Indochina and to the Nationalist Chinese in Formosa; these are not in any legal sense "allies."

In summary, from the standpoint of "armament mobilization" our associates in the free world fall roughly into three categories—the Rio Pact countries, the Atlantic Pact countries, plus Greece and Turkey, and certain of the countries of Asia.

The production of modern arms and the support of modern armed forces is an expensive business, forcing a great drain on the economy of any country.

Of our associates, only the North Atlantic Treaty countries possess the ability to produce modern military equipment. The remaining countries, if they are to have modern arms, must acquire them from the United States, Canada, or the countries of Western Europe, either by gift or by payment in foreign exchange. But since the military production capacity of the countries of Western Europe still falls far below their requirements to equip their own forces, there is at present no source of modern arms for the remainder of the free world other than the United States.

Turning to strategy of free world rearmament, it seems readily apparent that the countries of Latin America and of Asia are in an entirely different category from those of Western Europe. The former countries cannot hope to support modern military establishments adequate to repel the aggression of a great power. The best they can achieve is the military force necessary for internal police power, and it may require a considerable force—witness the Indochinese problem. They are dependent in considerable part for logistical support for any expeditionary forces on the United States or some other Western power.

The countries of Western Europe, on the other hand, have the productive potential to support modern armed forces, once these forces are equipped. They have the capability of contributing materially to the initial equipment. They have the capability within the foreseeable future of building the military power which, when backed by adequate American and Canadian strength in reserve across the Atlantic, will serve as a shield deterring aggression and, if necessary, repelling invasion.

Put very simply, our policy of arms aid assistance at present is to provide the countries of low productivity in Asia and South America with the arms essential for current operational requirements against Communism, for internal security, and (in the case of our Latin Allies) for taking over certain tasks which would otherwise require American manpower. We are providing our North Atlantic Treaty Allies with that portion of the initial equipment needed to arm ground, naval, and air forces adequate to hold Western Europe which they cannot provide for themselves. At the same time we propose to assist them with economic aid directed in considerable part to generating production of equipment by their own industry. This last policy lessens the demands on United States industry during the years of rearmament and provides a capability to maintain the forces, once they are raised and equipped. There are available to us three possible courses of action in regard to the mobilization of our Allies:

(1) We can surrender.

(2) We can take upon ourselves the entire burden of security for the United States, disregarding completely our friends in the rest of the world. Some people call this resigning ourselves to a "garrison state."

(3) We can undertake our security effort on a mutual basis. That is the way we have chosen.

The dollar is an inadequate yardstick in many human endeavors, but it is the best yardstick we have to use in quick analysis. Approximately ten billion dollars in a year sounds like a lot of money. It is only about 15 per cent of the budget of the Defense Department or 3 per cent of our national production, but it still is a lot of money. Measured in resources which count, in steel, in aluminum, in copper —perhaps even more in beef—it means a great deal.

I know some people ask, "What is the use of setting up armies over there when what actually will happen is that the Russians will come over here and bomb us or they will bomb the European cities, so that all this is really a waste of money?"

Of course, there is no clear-cut answer—either white or black (I hope certainly not black). We are doing our best. We are choosing or setting up the least bad solution—that is one way to put it—to a very clear threat to the security of the United States. Some people call it total survival of the free world, and our strategy is summed up in the very simple sentence that we are striving to build that strength in the North Atlantic area which deters aggression and if necessary will repel invasion of the North Atlantic area.

It should be fairly obvious to anybody who reads the newspapers that we do not, as of today, have the military power in being to repel invasion, to hold the line of the Iron Curtain. But we do, at the present time, have military power in being which is considered adequate to constitute some deterrent to aggression.

Some people think that our atomic advantage is diminishing. I will not comment or pass judgment on that.

Our objective is simply to build in as short a time as possible—and that amounts to a production and financial problem as much as a mobilization and training problem—additional military strength in Western Europe, and also in the United States, so that the power will exist to repel invasion. That gives us a very critical one or two years ahead.

Let me sum this up in a simple analogy. When the fire alarm rings, do you throw the baby out of the window because you are afraid you won't be able to walk down the stairs without slipping? Maybe you won't be able to walk down the stairs without slipping, but of course it is good common sense to try it first—before opening the window.

I suggest that in appraising our individual answers to the question, "Can we afford to mobilize our Allies?" we recognize that we are probably appraising the answer to the question, "How much can we afford to pay to live?" Then perhaps we can all agree that the question to be decided is not: "Can we afford it?" Rather the crucial questions are: "How much is necessary?" and "What are the most efficient plans and programs for doing the job?"

Economic Aspects

The primary objective of European rearmament, from the economic viewpoint, is to get the European governments to make two principal decisions: (1) to increase their military budgets considerably and (2) to adopt the measures of domestic economic policy necessary to the carrying out of those military budgets, i.e., diversion of resources from civilian to military use.

In terms of United States policy in Europe, there are two further but equally important considerations: (1) In the short run we have got to prevent the impact of this rearmament effort—increased defense spending and controls—from having serious effects on the political stability and morale in the countries concerned. (2) For the long run, we must take care not to hamper the economic growth of Europe as a whole or to undermine the European trading position in the world, so that Europe may, in time, be able again to become independent of American economic aid.

Quite obviously, in Europe as in the United States, the chief economic means of getting a rearmament effort going is to increase over-all production either by reëmployment of resources not at present employed or by increasing the productivity of resources already in use. There exists in continental Europe—particularly in Italy, Belgium, and Germany, and to quite a fair extent in France—a considerable amount of unused productive capacity in the form of short hours, unemployment, and unused plant in the metallurgical, the chemical, and the so-called engineering industries. Out of this untapped reservoir of additional economic output at least a part of the European rearmament can be covered.

I think, however, that it is most important in considering the economic aspects of the European military effort to concentrate attention on the problem of inflation or—to look at it another way—the problem of what kind of cuts in consumer spending (that is, consumer real income) are feasible in carrying out the defense effort.

To understand that problem, it is necessary to divide Western Europe into two groups of countries which can be expected to react differently—the northern countries and the principal continental countries.

(1) The northern countries, including Britain, Norway, and the Netherlands, have the kind of economy or society which is capable, to a considerable degree, of consumer sacrifice without serious political repercussions. For one thing, the national morale of those countries is reasonably sound. They are characterized by what is known as tax morality and a general willingness to conform to government controls. Again, the distribution of income is on the whole equitable, and taxes are highly progressive.

The effect of all these factors is that an increased national military budget or a new and tighter set of economic controls can be imposed without setting off any runaway price inflation and without creating inequities serious enough to cause insurmountable political problems.

These northern countries—particularly Britain—of course have, except for Norway, a higher real standard of living than do most of the continental countries. There has been a rapid increase in both consumption and productivity in recent years. It is the fact that the situation is not extremely inflationary to start with which makes it possible to impose this new burden without precipitating serious economic or political disturbances.

I do not mean to imply that we can expect the British Government, for instance, to cut the average standard of living or average consumption by anything like 10 per cent or 15 per cent. That is not at all likely. About the most we can expect is a small per-capita reduction. But even that would compare rather favorably with what can be expected in the continental countries. (I don't know what is going to happen to the American standard of living, but I doubt if it will be cut any more, proportionately, than the British.)

(2) The continental countries—principally France, Germany, and Belgium—no matter how dissimilar they may be in other respects, are alike in the factors that are important for the purposes of this discussion, i.e., those that determine their ability, or rather their inability, to withstand the impact of increased defense expenditure.

Among other things, there is a very low degree of confidence in the value of the money. A small degree of price inflation immediately sets off a rather rapid flight from the currency. Also, the tax structure is not progressive, which means that, as the supply of money and money incomes increase, there is no automatic dampening effect on inflation such as would occur in this country or the UK. Again, there is basically poor tax morality and an unwillingness or lack of sincere desire to conform to economic controls of any kind. Finally, the national morale generally is of a lower order.

In the light of all these factors, it would be extremely unrealistic to count on the continental countries for any cut in civilian consumption in absolute terms or even relative to national income. The effect of reëmployment in Germany, Italy, and to some extent France will be to increase production, but such production will tend to be taken up by consumption.

This matter of morale, on which so much depends economically, deserves a little further explanation. Why, for instance, are so many of these people apparently unwilling to meet their financial responsibilities through taxation to support their democratic governments? Is this inherent in their national traits, or does it reflect a real doubt in the power of their government to produce what they want, or is it still an outgrowth of the demoralization of the last war which they are coming out of slowly, or just what is the explanation?

Part of the answer lies in the history of some of the continental peoples. This attitude toward taxes and government regulation is no new phenomenon for many European countries. Despite their much longer history, as far as effective constitutional government is concerned, they are at a stage in their political evolution which is in many ways much less mature than ours. That is true with respect to France and Italy, just as it is even more true of the more backward, less-developed countries of Europe like Portugal and Spain. There is also the matter of the strength of national political cohesion and loyalty which obviously bears on the question of tax morality. Take the case of Italy. As a quite personal view, I would say that Italian national morale has never been really strong. There has never been real national cohesion in Italy. The morale of the Italian armies was weak in both world wars. Sectionalism, or regionalism, is a powerful force in Italian politics and even more so in Spain. But that is not the whole picture. I think there is also an important factor of demoralization of more recent origin, dating, say, from the first World War.

The situation in France is more complex. As far as national pride and national cohesion are concerned, France has undoubtedly suffered since the first World War. The German occupation in the second World War was particularly hard on France. There has been a gradual decline in nationalism, a loss of belief in the importance of France as a sovereign state. It is not unusual to hear sophisticated Frenchmen say there is no future for France as France, but only for Europe, and for France as a part of Europe.

The fact that national demoralization resulting from the impact of the second World War has played a big part is shown by what has happened in Germany. The pre-Hitler Germany was law-abiding, the people above all things paying their taxes, obeying the government, indeed loving, respecting, and fearing their government in a way we could never understand or feel in the Anglo-Saxon countries. Yet these same Germans now are famous for their disregard of regulations, for tax evasion, for their skeptical attitude toward the government.

It is not too difficult to understand why the Germans' respect for constituted authority, belief in Germany as a nation, is seriously weakened. There just is no real German state, at least as a recognized political unit. The Germans do not know where they are going or how things will develop. Being in the dark as to their political future, they feel most insecure.

On the other hand—crossing the channel—England did not lose the war. She won it. She was not occupied. The British people, when Britain was fighting alone, put on one of the most extraordinary demonstrations of national guts, national cohesion, that the world has seen in recent times. The British have every reason to be proud of what they did in the war.

If the British show signs of impatience with us and with their own problems, it is not through any deep loss of faith in themselves such as you see in the continental countries. They do undoubtedly feel upset that they are no longer the "top dog." They feel under our shadow, and they are not quite used to the idea. It will perhaps take them a long time to get used to it. But their national morale is still reasonably sound.

What this all adds up to in terms of the future is really the major question of Western European defense. Is it conceivable that the French will really fight? They did not fight in 1940; at least they did not fight well enough. My own opinion is that on the basis of fighting for France, for France only, the chances of France's fighting better in the future than she did in the second World War are not especially good. But if she can be brought to fight for some kind of United Europe which is in some kind of closer alliance with the United States and Britain, I think the chances are very good that we can expect of France the kind of morale on which real military strength depends.

I think the same can be said for the Western Germans and Italians. The German problem is particularly critical because the Western Germans are perhaps the only people in continental Europe who have a real political alternative to coöperating with the United States: they can stay neutral, playing "footsy" with Eastern Germany and the Soviets, and there are not a few Germans who would like to play that sort of game.

To get back to the economic picture, the general view is that it would definitely be unwise to try to finance the military effort by a sharp reduction in European investment. Some cuts will be necessary, but any attempt to slice investment to the bone would only be storing up serious trouble for later. The present defense program is not intended to be an all-out effort—either in Western Europe or in America. The objective is simply a rearmament effort consistent with maintenance of the economic strength which has been gained in Europe, rather than to put Europe back into the role of international pauper in our effort to rearm her. Then we all will be better able to meet the all-out effort if and when it is called for.

Accordingly, our program must be made up of a large component of military grants and a small component of economic aid. I think that such a program reflects basically sound specialization. Western

Europe can best provide most of the manpower for armed forces and the financing to support that manpower, take care of the needed construction and maintenance, and so on. The United States can best provide most of the military equipment required for those forces, as well as for its own forces. I think that such a division of labor makes sense economically speaking, so long as Europe's ability to spend for military purposes is limited. If Europe were to put the major part of its effort into production of military equipment, it would be unable to cover the costs of raising, training, and supporting military forces and the costs of construction and maintenance—costs which are necessarily locally incurred in Europe.

I do not mean to imply that there will be no military production in Europe. There will be, and it will increase in percentage terms very much in the course of the next couple of years. We are, of course, making every effort to see that it does increase. But the fact remains that by far the largest share of the military equipment will have to come from us.

As for the economic component of our program, it is small but critical. Without such aid European production would be much lower. Not only would Europe be unable to maintain the production necessary for a high-level economy; it would also be unable to supply the goods necessary for export; it would be unable to divert the chemical industry necessary for arms production; and so on.

Raw Materials

It is important to remember that the total foreign aid program is only about 15 per cent of our total security program, and the security program itself is not a tremendous effort. As a matter of fact, the total expected increase in production from pre-Korea up to the time when we reach peak output will probably ensure as much for the civilian use of this country as we had before Korea, if not more.

Again, the economic aid program of seven and a half billion or ten billion dollars a year is only about one-fourth of what we spent annually for lend-lease during the second World War.

We must recognize, however, that in one sense the dollar dimensions mean very little. The necessary dollars we can, and are, providing. But all our production is based on raw materials, and their availability is a matter of reciprocal exchange. The value to us of the raw materials which we must get from other countries is simply incalculable.

Many people think of such dramatic substitutes as nylon for silk and synthetic rubber for natural rubber and, therefore, are inclined to assume we are becoming increasingly independent in sources of supply for raw materials. As a matter of fact, the exact opposite is true. We have become more and more—and unless or until longer range plans for substitutes are worked out will continue to be to a high degree—dependent on foreign sources of supply.

In the case of many major and now critical materials, we were net exporters before the war. Now we import them. Imports are an increasing percentage of our consumption. For example, imports of lumber are 3 per cent of our consumption; petroleum products, 9 per cent; iron ore, 9 per cent; oil, 15 per cent; copper, one-third; lead, one-third; zinc, 15 per cent. There are several reasons for this change:

(1) To a large extent we depleted many of our resources in the second World War. Copper, which we used to export in huge amounts, we now must import heavily, simply because many of our mines were worked out during the war.

(2) Between 1939 and today there has been a terrifically increased expansion in the production of metal items—as high as 150 per cent—for machinery and equipment, automobiles, and consumer durable goods taken as a whole.

(3) There has also been a growing demand, as the result of technological requirements, for the nonferrous alloys not found to any large extent in this country, such as uranium, tungsten, cobalt, nickel; and there has been a great expansion in chemical production since the second World War. The development of synthetic rubber, for instance, itself takes large amounts of chemicals; and plastics, though also substituting for rubber, likewise use up chemicals. For some of these chemicals we are either dependent on foreign sources of supply or else we are tending to shift from being a large exporter to being a balanced user.

The development of this critical situation has been going on for some years, but it really accelerated in 1951. Let me briefly trace the steps:

(1) During the second World War our production was very high, and both France and Germany were, for example, out of business as importers. That condition continued into 1946 and 1947, with the importing countries still prostrate or trying to get back on their feet. We were continuing to use for civilian consumption many resources and supplies.

(2) Then during 1947 and 1948 we had a slight recession in this country, and with the drop in consumption of durable equipment, our requirements for copper and many other critical materials declined; but by this time the foreign countries were back on their feet. During this period we used large amounts of materials that had accumulated here during the war.

(3) Soon we began to expand our production again very rapidly, and Europe remained prosperous. We got by in 1950 only by drawing to a dangerous extent on the stocks of critical materials in this country.

(4) And now we are trying to impose on our heavy civilian consumption an armament program which requires very large amounts of these critical metals—for example, nickel and cobalt for jet engines and for armor plate. In some instances, the military requirements of these items amount to 50 per cent of our normal civilian consumption.

Our share of the world production of these items on which we are dependent for outside supply has gone up enormously since 1939. Newsprint has gone from 65 per cent to 90 per cent; iron ore has gone from 35 per cent to 50 per cent; cobalt is up to 80 per cent. So understandably there is a considerable resentment among foreigners of the extent to which the United States tends to grab all these materials from sources of supply which they consider to be normally theirs on the basis of prewar experience.

Unilateral action on our part has only created difficulties of this sort. We tried to shut off United States exports of copper; consequently, foreign countries, desperate for supplies, went to our outside sources. To get what they needed to increase production, they tended to bid up the price beyond what our businessmen could pay under price controls. The net result was that copper stopped flowing into the country. So we have had to go ahead and make allocations against what we achieved in cutting down on exports.

In the last war our Raw Materials Board did most of the work in allocating the supply of copper throughout the world in coöperation with Britain and Canada. We were rather rough with neutrals, and we did not have to be concerned with Western Europe then. Many of the actions taken were quite arbitrary. For example, we negotiated very favorable (to us) contracts with the Latin American countries, whereby they agreed to accept dollar payments during the war; the idea was that they could use their dollars to buy capital equipment after the war. But subsequently, when our price controls were removed, they found that their dollars did not go very far in buying capital equipment. Naturally, they are reluctant to enter into a deal of that kind again.

As a result there have been set up a series of international materials conferences with representatives from the United States, UK, Italy, France, Brazil, Canada, Australia, and India. In addition, the central group sponsors a number of materials conferences in individual countries, with representatives from the major producing and consumer countries. The United States is represented in every case, and the balance of the representation varies according to the product—for example, Australia would be on the wool conference, Bolivia on the tin conference, and so on.

These conferences are not a set of operating agencies. Their only function is to review the situation and to make recommendations to the governments as to what action should be taken to increase the production of materials and to allocate the supplies on a world-wide basis in accordance with some standard of prewar consumption. To date, none of these conferences has progressed far enough to reach the point at which basic decisions have been made, so I do not know how this more complicated system of allocating metals and agricultural materials on a world-wide basis will work out.

One of the stumbling blocks to the satisfactory work of these committees has been the United States' stockpile position. We tend to think of our stockpiles as second in importance only to military requirements. But other countries feel differently. They say that if we have a stockpile, they should have a stockpile; that, of course, intensifies the shortage of these critical materials. Or else they say that if we want to build up stockpiles, that is our business so long as we do it out of allocations made to us in proportion to prewar consumption so that we will not be drawing on the world pool of materials but on the supply which is allocated to us.

To repeat, the situation is very much more complicated than in the second World War. We have to consider not only our Allies but also neutral countries now. We can no longer be arbitrary as we were then.

Political Aspects

The importance of Europe to us today should be at the basis of any United States policy toward that part of the world. It is imperative that we not be governed merely by such concepts as our responsibilities to Europe, our common ties, and so on. In this case, do not our ties and historical associations and our interests all coincide?

People all too often think of Europe's importance to us only in terms of positive factors—what Europe can add to our resources, what manpower Europe can contribute to the common cause. I should like to suggest that aside from the positive importance of Europe, which itself is not always sufficiently understood, there is also its negative importance—i.e., what Europe does not contribute to the Soviet Union and which it would contribute if we lost it. This aspect would have even greater importance.

Just consider what would happen if Europe should fall under the Soviet sway. It would be able to supply the USSR's greatest need, skilled labor. For Europe still constitutes the largest pool of skilled labor in the world. It would supply other needs too. For example, European resources would more than double Soviet coal and aluminum output, triple its steel and electric power production, make its shipbuilding capacity greater than that of the British Isles.

Nazi Germany in the last war demonstrated all too clearly how an occupying power can exploit such resources. The Nazi accomplishments in this field would look like child's play compared to what the Soviets would get out of Europe with their methods. Along with the control of Europe proper, control of the Asiatic land mass and of

Northern Africa would doubtless fall to the Soviets; we could not count on saving them. That would give the Soviets not only Europe and all of Europe's sources of strategic raw materials but much more in addition. We would be left with the southern half of Africa and the American continent.

Some people talk about "going it alone." Anybody can go it alone, but anybody can always commit suicide, too. I submit that any policy which would willfully increase the odds against us is not using everyday, plain horse sense. Furthermore, we must recognize that there is a limit to what one hundred and thirty million Americans and thirteen million Canadians can do.

No policy relating to the defense of Europe can overlook certain political and psychological hazards. First and foremost there is a lack of conviction in Europe that the security goal is actually within our reach. In that lies the answer to the familiar question about the Europeans' will to resist. I think it is as simple as that. We cannot expect any country to have a national will to suicide. But, by the same token, as the sense of power becomes stronger, the will to resist becomes greater. We have a hump to get over; once we are over it, with each succeeding step we shall see the will to resist growing by leaps and bounds.

There is another major hindrance, namely the brittleness of the financial system in the European countries. The people have gone through two generations with one inflation after another. Inflation in Europe is less economic than it is with us, and is much more psychological. For example, the limit of the banknote issue of the Bank of France has only to be announced, and immediately an inflation psychology is generated. Because of past experience with inflation, any development associated with inflations has much more harmful effects in these countries than it would have elsewhere.

I have just come back from a much too rapid tour of several continental European countries, and I was quite unpleasantly disturbed to hear in all quarters of the damage that has already been done in the last few months by the resumption of the inflationary spiral. The implementation of defense plans for Europe is further retarded by the quasi-disappearance of public credit on the continent. As a result, the only means available to the European countries for the financing of their part of our joint defense effort is taxation. Public borrowing must be eliminated as a practical source.

Another stumbling block is the European inferiority complex, which has resulted from the thumping defeat that our present Allies on the continent suffered in 1940. This inferiority complex is gradually being remedied, but it is still there, and it is accompanied by a tremendous respect and envy for United States power. There is the temptation and tendency to look toward the American giant as the only effective source of security for Europe and to belittle the results of European self-help.

At the same time, there is a sharp psychological problem to overcome. The Europeans have unwittingly absorbed much of the Communists' propaganda. One will hear in all quarters, including strongly anti-Communist circles, "We don't want to be Americanized any more than we want to be Sovietized." It is not just something which is mentioned as a theoretical attitude; it represents a very real feeling, and I have been struck on the occasion of my last trip by its growth during the past couple of years.

In this connection we must be careful to retain the goodwill of all non-Communist circles. We must respect their pride and self-respect. This means that we must be careful not to act as if we thought of ourselves as one favored nation, in a category all unto itself, which can do what it will, when it will, and with scant attention to the interests or feelings of our friends.

Europe must and can do more. But I think we also should retain our balance and should bear in mind what it has done during the past two years or so. We have a long road ahead. Pride in the great distance we have already come should not blind us to the great distance we still have to go.

Conclusion

Above all, we must be realistic. When considering questions such as that of tax morality, for example, we must remember the difference between our per-capita income and standard of living and that of the taxpayer in, say, Italy. The Italian lira that goes for taxes means the loss of some bread that would otherwise go into the stomach—not, as it might mean with us, less gin for Martinis or getting along with the old car for a few more months. That makes quite a difference in the enthusiasm with which people pay taxes.

Or take the question of whether the Europeans whom we are helping will respond if and when the crisis develops. Some people cite the fact that the other members of the United Nations are contributing only 10 per cent of the Korean effort, but that 10 per cent figure is highly misleading because it represents only a part of the total picture. As a matter of fact, the French have suffered in Indochina more casualties—in proportion to their population—than we have in Korea. They have in Indochina over 150,000 of their best officers and men, and the war there is using up a third of their military budget.

The British are fighting in Malaya to protect the rubber production which we are using for civilian as well as military uses. Granted they are getting paid for the rubber; the important fact is that it is being produced and is not falling into the hands of the "Commie" bandits. Moreover, up until recently the British have been spending a greater percentage of their total resources on defense than we were.

I think it is beside the point to say that France and Britain are merely defending their colonial possessions and that in supporting them we are keeping these colonies from gaining their independence. The French colonies, like the English, have been gradually changing, and Indochina is moving toward sovereignty equal to that of the British Dominions. At the present time, the French and the Indochinese are fighting against what amounts to Communist invasion; the struggle there, as in Europe, is a part of the total defense against Communist aggression. Certainly Soviet control of Indochina, which is what would happen if the French left Indochina to its own devices, would be a less desirable alternative for the Indochinese people than the present evolution of the colony to an independent state.

The shrivelled-up little America we would have after abandoning everyone else who shares our objectives and heritage and aspirations is about the most un-American concept I can imagine. It is the kind of thinking that said, when we reached a gross national production of one hundred billion dollars, we had just about denuded our country of all its resources and capabilities. In the twelve months from 1950 to 1951 we increased output 10 per cent. Our normal national productivity has passed the three hundred billion dollar mark. We are going on up, according to Charles Wilson, toward the three hundred and fifty billion dollar mark. We cannot keep up that kind of pace indefinitely, according to Wilson, but it is something to be proud of and to have faith in.

And here is another reason for pride. What do we do with the output? Do we keep it all for ourselves and get fatter and slower and less and less American, or do we share it on a sensible, practical, businesslike, partnership basis?

What are the other countries doing to merit this? To use an analogy, they are really people who have just got out of the hospital, and we are putting packs on their backs and guns and grenades in their hands. We are asking them to make bazookas rather than cars, airbases rather than bridges. Despite their weak condition, they have shown that they are willing to take on these tasks, for they recognize the present danger as clearly as we. This is a common fight. Together we are trying to maintain something that we all cherish—our human dignity and our priceless freedom. We can do it if we will.

RELATIONS WITH LATIN AMERICA

Edward G. Miller, Jr.

Few people in this country realize the importance of Latin America to the business of the United States as a whole. Last year 35 per cent of all United States imports came from Latin America, and 27 per cent of our exports went to Latin America. These exports totaled approximately 2.7 billion dollars, which was very nearly as much as our total of exports to Europe. United States exports to Western Europe in 1950 were valued at roughly 2.9 billion dollars, just two hundred and ten million dollars more than our Latin American exports, and nearly two billion dollars of United States trans-Atlantic exports were paid for out of Marshall Plan funds.

Similarly Latin America is extremely important as a United States foreign investment. At the end of the year 1949, United States private investment in Latin America totaled over 5.8 billion dollars. Dollar investments have flowed to Latin America since the war at an unprecedented rate. In the three years from 1947 through 1949, 1.7 billion dollars was added to the total of private United States investment in Latin America. The 1950 year-end figures are not yet complete, but it is safe to say we now have well over six billion dollars invested in Latin America. In comparison, private American investment outside the Western Hemisphere totals something over seven billion dollars.

The scope of the economic involvement of the United States in Latin America becomes particularly impressive when it is realized that the population of Latin America represents less than 7 per cent of the population of the world, having recently, like the United States population, passed the one hundred and fifty million mark.

Even more impressive is the fact that not only is the population comparatively small to have assumed such an important role for

NOTE: Mr. Miller is Assistant Secretary of State for Inter-American Affairs.

United States business, but this importance has been attained even though these countries are still, in view of their great potential, only on the threshold of their industrial development. For example, in 1949 the national income of the United States was about nine times as great as the combined national incomes of all of the Latin American countries.

Comparing the United States and Mexico, in 1949 the Mexican per-capita income was the equivalent of $121 when the United States per-capita income was $1,453. There were 5.5 passenger cars in Mexico per 1,000 population in 1949. There were 243 per 1,000 in the United States.

But perhaps the most significant aspect of what we have been discussing from the standpoint of United States business for the future is that Latin America is not static; that economic growth is proceeding at a very rapid pace, even in relation to this country. To my mind, this fact—that Latin America is developing at a fast pace—is the main fact in thinking ahead for business. In the case of Mexican automobiles, for instance, according to Mexican Government statistics, motor vehicle registrations have climbed 140 per cent since 1937. Registrations have increased 50 per cent in the United States in the same period.

The last twenty years have brought tremendous economic growth in Latin America, and in many ways more progress has occurred during this period than in the entire nineteenth century, at least in regard to industrial and commercial development.

It is reasonable to assume that this rate of growth will be maintained in Latin America, provided always that the necessary imports of capital equipment will be forthcoming during the period of shortages imposed by the present emergency. I will go further and say that since development in itself promotes development, the rate of growth in Latin America should be even greater in the future, all other things being equal. A necessary consequence is that the standard of living of Latin America and the per-capita purchasing power should continually increase in relation to United States levels. An important factor in this connection is the progressive development of efficient labor forces in these countries as new industries are created.

And, of course, as we all know from the history of this country, more growth means more opportunities.

A second fact to be remembered is that the growth which has occurred in Latin America is to a large extent the result of a factor which was not operative in the economic growth of the United States. In this country, expansion of our economy has been fairly constant throughout our history and, except for periods of war and national emergency, has been a more or less "natural" process—individual initiative applied in an uncoördinated way to the development of resources. In Latin America there is no such record of steady growth. Rather, for a long time many of the economies were relatively static in regard to industrial development, their principal effort having been devoted to agriculture and real estate. In the last twenty years in most countries a radical change has occurred, and industrial development has surged ahead suddenly. This surge has come about to an important degree by popular demand. The people in Latin America, as in other parts of the world, are not content with their lot, and they are no longer apathetic about it. They want a greater share of the good things of life. They want their countries to be prosperous, to offer them greater opportunities for employment and broader horizons for their children.

These are pressures to which the governments of Latin America are subjected, and, by and large, these governments have become increasingly responsive to the will of the people. I think they will become even more responsive in the future, for the critical problem for governments in many Latin American countries during the next few decades may well be whether or not living standards and social development will advance rapidly enough to keep discontent from boiling over into blind destruction or from being utilized by international Communism for its own ruthless and antidemocratic ends.

What can be seen now in many countries of the hemisphere are determined and conscious efforts to bring about economic expansion. In some cases government agencies have been formed to cope with the problem, as in the case of the Chilean Development Corporation and the Mexican Nacional Financiera. In Puerto Rico, where the problem is the same as in the independent countries of Latin America, we have the notable example of Governor Muñoz Marin's so-called "Operation Bootstrap," where the government has not only taken direct action in stimulating industrial activity but has also sought to create the conditions which attract private capital investment from the United States.

It might be said parenthetically that our government has seen fit on its own part to help economic expansion in Latin America through means appropriate for governmental activity. Our programs of technical and economic coöperation through such agencies as the Institute of Inter-American Affairs, the Export-Import Bank, and the International Bank are too well known to be dealt with here. I shall only say that the activities of these institutions have been directed toward providing basic public services and participating in programs of basic development which in turn help promote private activity.

Recently our government's efforts in the field of economic development have been subject to a searching review by a distinguished group of citizens under the chairmanship of Mr. Nelson Rockefeller. Their conclusions have been embodied in a report which, in substance, recommends a considerable intensification of this type of activity. The report also recommends new methods by which our government can help stimulate the increased flow of private capital abroad. These include tax incentive measures, investment treaties, and limited guarantees by the Export-Import Bank of specific investment projects. These are all measures which have been receiving active study by our government. A special value of the report is that it rationalizes the relative participation of public and private endeavor in the expansion of economic activity in underdeveloped areas.

There are, then, two main facts to be borne in mind in regard to the future in Latin America. First, that economic growth in this area has been proceeding rapidly and will probably continue even more rapidly; and, secondly, that this trend is in large measure the result of a new awakening and demand by the people for more economic activity.

Naturally, these trends are characterized by certain aspects which are not entirely in accord with classical doctrines of international economics. In a number of cases we have seen the creation of new industries which are economically unsound to the extent that they depend upon undue tariff protection or are uneconomic from the standpoint of accessibility of raw materials. There has been in some countries a tendency toward governmental ownership of industry, where, again, the results may be uneconomic from the standpoint of such indices as productivity per man hour. In still other countries the climate may be hostile for the entrance of foreign capital. The people and the government of the country concerned may wish to reserve for themselves exclusively the task of developing their resources. There are numerous other problems of a similar nature which could be enumerated.

In considering the factors affecting private business in Latin America, what should be the attitude of United States business? First, of course, there is no question that tremendous opportunities exist in the hemisphere—opportunities for constructive assistance on the part of United States business in the sound development of the economy of these countries. On the other hand, the conditions under which foreign capital is going to be allowed to participate in these opportunities will depend upon the freely exercised sovereign will of the twenty independent countries which comprise this area of the free world.

We in our government, or you in business, may not approve of some of the economic theories and practices which we see in other countries. We may think they are unwise even from the standpoint of the long-range self-interest of the other country. We may deplore them in speeches and resolutions. We—and now I am speaking of the government alone—may do our best to bring about better understanding of our motives, of our views as to the functions of responsible capital investment in the modern world; we may and do try through representations in individual cases and through our efforts to negotiate economic treaties to bring about an improved climate for private activity. We have consistently pointed out that the problem of development is not one that can be solved by government activities, that true and balanced development can only happen by permitting full play to the forces of private initiative and skills, both domestic and foreign. We have emphasized and we shall continue to emphasize that economic assistance from the United States Government can be more effectively brought to bear in countries where these conditions exist.

But I repeat: The terms and conditions under which foreign capital will be admitted into another country are up to that country. We as a government will most scrupulously respect the sovereign right of each juridically equal nation of the hemisphere to run its own affairs. We in the Department of State—as much as we may admire the achievements of individual enterprise—cannot undertake the functions of sponsors of United States capital investment. Unlike the Soviet Union, the United States is not out to impose its systems on other countries.

Therefore, it seems to me that the wisest attitude businessmen can assume in thinking about investment in Latin America is to try to see things as they are and to work within the existing scheme of things. This may mean that business will stay entirely out of situations that are too precarious. In other cases it will mean putting up with certain difficulties of the kinds which I have enumerated, but I suppose that nowhere in the world are the conditions for business exactly what business would like to see, and that goes for the laws of our own Federal Union and its forty-eight component states.

This also means, I think, that the most effective contribution to a favorable climate for private investment is for American business, both here and abroad, to show that it represents the best system in the world—the best system not only from the standpoint of productivity but in the light of the desire of people everywhere to get a better share of the good things of life. All business, in short, must prove itself. You and I believe that the United States private enterprise is the best system, but it does not follow automatically that other people—people with different habits and traditions—will necessarily think as we do about this particular aspect of our national life. The only way that other people can be brought to believe in this system is for them to be convinced that it works, and that it works not only here but in their country, whatever it may be. How, specifically, can business prove itself in this way? There would be no point in my lecturing men, who have wider experience than I have in this field, so I suggest that the best guides are found in the records of the American enterprises which have had the greatest success in Latin America.

In the first place, almost without exception, if they have done well, they have abided by the rules and regulations of the other country. This may seem an obvious precept, almost too obvious to mention. However, real doubt from time to time is engendered abroad as to the willingness of American capital to live within the rules of the game in a particular country.

Secondly, the American interests which have been most esteemed and in general have been most fairly treated in Latin America are those which have shown a genuine concern for the general welfare of the other country. It seems to have been particularly, and understandably, difficult for Americans to see eye-to-eye with Latin American governments on what constitutes "general welfare" where government-sponsored development programs were under way. But to date, nothing has been achieved by bucking the plans of a sovereign government. American enterprise has made great contributions to the development of national steel enterprises in Brazil and Chile, and in the latter country over one hundred fifty American technicians, furnished by American companies, are now contributing to the welfare of the people and to our own relations with that country. In Colombia an American oil company whose concession has expired is assisting the Colombian Government to continue to operate the concession. These examples will go far to promote the interest of private enterprise as a whole.

In some cases great strides have been made by improving public relations of American enterprises in general and labor relations in particular. A number of American enterprises have decided they can no longer content themselves with the claim that they pay better wages than other countries. At this point, personnel management programs and similar devices prove to be very valuable aids to successful operation. The effort that is being put forth by certain American interests to apply in Latin America the labor-management procedures which we have developed here is, to my mind, the most worthwhile effort of all.

It would be well to bear in mind that the interests of capital and labor, far from being irreconcilable, are in the true sense of the word identical. One of the most eloquent statements of this case is by Mr. William Green, President of the American Federation of Labor, who on October 13, 1950, said:

> "Communism has sought to make a bogey of capitalism by painting it as a system of exploitation and oppression, imposed on the many for the benefit of the few. They preach that capitalism is doomed, since it bears within it the seeds of its own destruction.
>
> Trade Unionism, on the other hand, has demonstrated to the world that there has never been anything wrong with capitalism that higher wages and shorter hours could not cure. It has shown that capitalism can mean more democracy, not less, and that it can bring material, cultural and social progress and improvement to the many rather than the few. Modern trade unionism is an outgrowth of industrial capitalism and has provided the mechanism whereby the fruits of capitalism have been distributed over an ever-widening area of the populace. Far from being foredoomed, capitalism has thus borne within it the seeds of its own salvation. This is the revolutionary message that American labor is placing before the workers of the world today."

If, in their Latin American operations, United States businessmen can foster that type of labor philosophy, we have no reason to fear for the future of free enterprise, both local and foreign, in Latin America. And it must be obvious to anyone who has been in Latin America that American concerns, if they are given the chance and if they will, can speed the growth of democratic labor leadership. It is fortunately true that attention to labor relations and personnel problems is coming to be another characteristic of those United States companies in Latin America which have the most promising future. They abide by local laws, they evidence a broader concern than the short-range welfare of their own enterprises, and they put into practice at least some of the lessons in labor-management relations which business has learned here at home.

There are other developments which I think we should hope will become characteristic. There are the number of cases in which

United States enterprises are working very hard to develop responsible local management and to reduce the number of United States citizens occupying top managerial positions, as well as top technical positions. There are the signs of increasing interest in incentive and bonus plans, as well as private retirement plans along the lines of those which have been successful in this country.

Also, American enterprises abroad are becoming more and more aware of the advantages of stock participation on the part of citizens of the other country. The enlightened self-interest involved in this type of program is evident when it is realized that one of the principal obstacles to development in Latin America has been the unavailability of local risk capital. It is all too evident that one of the principal deterrents to economic progress in other countries is a tendency to invest in real estate or family businesses and to expect a rate of return on capital investment far higher than our own investors and many times higher than equity investors expect here. It is encouraging, therefore, to see an American-owned public utility in Brazil currently financing part of the local currency costs of a major expansion program through sales of common stock to small investors who are served by the company.

Finally, American businessmen abroad are becoming more flexible and are learning increasingly to adjust to the requirements of the local scene and to the shifts which occur from time to time. They are becoming more farsighted and are learning to keep on the move.

In substance, the lesson which American business abroad is teaching us is that business abroad must act as part of the local community, not as an absentee-owned organization interested only in deriving profit, particularly not as an organization seeking "hit-and-run" profits from its enterprise. The entire scope of our relations with our neighbors is helped by such farsighted ventures as the Pan American School of Agriculture at Zamorano in Honduras, which is supported by the United Fruit Company, and the work of the Rockefeller Foundation in many countries of this hemisphere.

I hope what I have said will not be understood as a government spokesman urging American capital to go abroad or urging other countries to accept American capital. Private capital will move only of its own free will—that is, only if the investor finds that the risks in a particular situation are compensated by the opportunities over the long pull. There are still many opportunities for investment within the United States, which will naturally have a higher priority for the investor if the attractiveness of a situation outside the country is less than the hazards with which that situation is encumbered.

In other words, while it is true that all United States business abroad must prove itself to other countries, by the same token the other countries must show a real understanding of the problems of business. In some countries, even those which allege a desire for foreign capital, and even where American private investment has made great contributions to the general welfare, the conditions do not exist which are essential to attract American investment away from the investment opportunities which this country still presents and will always present. So long as there is discrimination in foreign countries, so long as foreign companies are made the butt of local political maneuvers, there will naturally be skepticism in the business community of this country in regard to any country in which such practices exist. In these cases American capital will not go.

The problem of private capital working abroad is, finally, one which depends upon mutual confidence. In many countries excellent progress has been made in establishing a climate favorable for private initiative. In some countries of the hemisphere the requisite mutual confidence is today a reality. In others it exists to a lesser extent. In some it does not exist at all. In thinking ahead for business, the great challenge is to prove over the long pull that the countries with confidence in United States private investment are following the right approach from the standpoint of their own self-interest.

PART II

INTERNAL PROBLEMS

THE PROBLEM OF INFLATION

Emerson P. Schmidt, Stanley H. Ruttenberg, and David M. Wright

A Business Point of View

Currently there is more public interest in inflation than there is in the defense program itself.

Webster defines inflation as a "disproportionate and relatively sharp and sudden increase in the quantity of money or credit or both, relative to the amount of goods available for purchase. Inflation always produces a rise in the price level."

In popular language and even in some policy-making circles, Webster's definition has been telescoped together to read, "Inflation *is* a rise in the price level."

This change in meaning has slipped into the language almost unnoticed, with some serious effects. A symptom has taken the place of the disease. And it is not surprising to find some groups advocating treatment of the symptom (price increases) by direct means (price controls), with a logic somewhat akin to immersing a fevered patient in icewater and letting it go at that.

In spite of this popular confusion, most responsible groups and persons are recognizing more and more that inflation is primarily a monetary phenomenon and that therefore the basic treatment for inflation must address itself to money and its use.

We have come a long way in our understanding of boom-and-bust, inflation, and price controls since the loose finance of the 1930's and the period of the second World War. During the first World War there was no popular support and little support from respon-

NOTE: Mr. Schmidt is Economist for the United States Department of Commerce; Mr. Ruttenberg is Director of the Department of Education and Research, CIO; and Mr. Wright is Professor, James Wilson School of Economics, University of Virginia.

Mr. Schmidt, Mr. Ruttenberg, and Mr. Wright are responsible, in that order, for the business, labor, and economist's viewpoints.

sible groups and individuals for a strict pay-as-we-go war-financing policy. Today, with few exceptions, pay-as-we-go is at least a *part* of everybody's "defense mobilization program." This represents gratifying progress in economic literacy.

More economists, many bankers, and others have been concerned over the "loose financial way of life" practiced by the Administration and particularly the United States Treasury in recent years. The North Korean aggression caught us in the midst of upward price pressures. Wholesale prices had been rising since the end of 1949; consumer prices started rising in March 1950. Thus the Korean aggression, followed by a stampede to get wage increases and anticipatory buying on the part of housewives and businessmen, built a boom upon an expanding economy.

From June to December 1950, commercial bank loans increased from 44.8 billion dollars to nearly 53 billion dollars—a net addition of eight billion dollars in only half a year. At an annual rate this was an increase of 35 per cent. Consumer credit during the same period rose from about 17.7 billion dollars to over twenty billion dollars—nearly 13.5 per cent. Mortgage real estate credit continued to expand at a rapid rate. In the same period demand deposits, our chief form of money, increased from about eighty-five billion dollars to over 93.2 billion dollars. During this period the total money supply (currency plus demand deposits) jumped upward from about 110 billion dollars to over 118 billion dollars—some four billion dollars above the previous postwar peak. Furthermore, the rate of use of the money supply (velocity of money turnover) had been rising steadily and is continuing to do so.

In the face of this expansion of the money supply, it is not surprising that the power of money spending has been reflected in a rise of wholesale prices from 157 (1926 = 100) in June 1950 to over 183 in early 1951, or almost 16 per cent. Meantime, retail or consumer prices have risen only from 170 in June 1950 (1935–1939 = 100) to about 185 in April 1951.

While these price increases are not solely attributable to the increase in credit and the money supply, there is a correspondence in direction and size of the movements; we are justified, therefore, in recognizing a causal connection. Wage increases, rising costs of replacing inventories, higher prices for replacement and expansion of capital equipment, and strong markets for goods—all these work together to encourage bank-loan expansion.

But if banks had not or could not have expanded loans and the money supply, all these upward pressures would have been substantially reduced.

In spite of this picture, the Secretary of the Treasury, in a speech made in January 1951, reaffirmed what in effect must be a "loose" monetary policy. I think the Treasury Department had a very bad case. It took the position that its cheap-money policy, the fixed-interest pattern, had nothing to do with inflation. Interest, claimed Mr. Snyder, was such a small cost of doing business that the raising of the interest rate would have no effect. Well, whoever the men are who write his speeches, they just do not know what they are talking about. Nobody has ever argued that a minor rise in the interest rate *per se* would slough off enough borrowing to stamp out inflation; the argument is rather that by restoring the power of the Federal Reserve System over commercial bank reserves, tightening up the reserve position, it can be made difficult or impossible for banks to loan money.

Academic and industrial economists and—much to their credit—bankers and others turned the heat on the United States Treasury and forced the decision. Perhaps more quickly than we had a right to expect, the United States Treasury and the Federal Reserve System announced "an accord" on March 3, 1951, which is likely to go down in recent history as the most important monetary decision of our time.[1]

This decision led to withdrawal of Federal Reserve support of a fixed-interest rate pattern, a prompt increase in interest rates, and, in the ensuing months, the cutting off of some marginal borrowing. But, far more important, it put to an end the rapid conversion of federal debt into bank credit. Presumably it restored the Federal

[1] For a more comprehensive analysis of the monetary basis of, and remedies for inflation, see Chamber of Commerce of the United States of America, *Economic Policies for National Defense* (March 1951).

Reserve System's power to control bank reserves, which is the key to the control of credit.

Almost immediately insurance companies and many other financial institutions found their lending plans overcommitted. New commitments were slowed down. They were no longer able to dump their government bonds on the market without a loss.

Meantime, of course, the control of installment and real estate credit provided for by the Defense Production Act of 1950 was beginning to show its effects. Only 88,000 new houses were started in April 1951 as against 133,000 in April 1950. Durable goods began to pile up on the shelves. Inventories of new and used cars began to mount. By May 1951 some automobile manufacturers closed down for "readjustments."

Some people question the effectiveness of the Voluntary Credit Restraint Program instituted in March 1951. First of all, let me point out that the program is somewhat mislabeled. It is in fact not strictly voluntary. (As Dr. Wright has so ably pointed out in his famous book, *Democracy and Progress*,[2] you do not have to use legal restraints in order to hem in people. You can do it by persuasion, by strong argument, or by shaming them.) This program is a very powerful legalized program, and it is, in my judgment, quite effective.

Ordinarily, voluntary self-restraint is something we cannot rely on. If a man was offered a job in a competing company at five thousand dollars a year more, and he decided that it really represented a desirable change, but for the sake of the national interest, in order not to increase disposable income in the national economy, he should turn the job down, he would be "quite a guy." You would not expect him to turn the offer down voluntarily. Similarly I think that ordinarily it would be unfair to expect bankers to restrain credit very much on a voluntary basis. If a customer comes in and asks for credit, which he is good for, but it is not granted and he feels that he has not been given proper treatment, he will walk across the street or into the next county, or he will go to the government; and

[2] David McCord Wright, *Democracy and Progress* (New York, The Macmillan Company, 1948).

if some other banker does not lend him money, maybe the government will.

But the program we are discussing has more teeth in it. It is a very highly organized program with a national credit restraint committee, with regional restraint committees, and with a whole lot of tie-ins with lending institutions, including the savings banks and the insurance companies, plus not only general directives as to what are good loans in terms of the inflationary situation and what are bad loans, but three separate bulletins dealing with different phases of credit expansion.

Mr. Wilson wrote letters to every governor and to the mayors of all the leading cities, urging them to drop recreational projects and a number of other kinds of projects including soldiers' bonuses. I know that in West Virginia a sixty-seven million dollar bond issue for soldiers' bonuses was a complete flop because Washington had urged investment bankers not to bid for that kind of bonds. That is perhaps an extreme case, but nevertheless it illustrates how the "Voluntary" Credit Restraint Program works.

In view of what I have just said, it will not be surprising that I do not favor a compulsory saving plan for consumers as a way to restrain inflation. I do not feel it is needed. Moreover, I do not approve of the idea of forcing people to do things they do not want to do when it is not necessary to force them. America stands for a minimum of pushing people around. That is one of the great concepts of the American way of life for which we are fighting. Of course in emergencies we have to take measures that we do not normally like, but to reiterate what I said before, it is not necessary this time—at least up to now. If the American people get the feeling that the government really means business about pay-as-you-go and maintenance of the purchasing power of the dollar, they will save. Especially as goods begin to disappear, goods they really want, and as quality deteriorates, they will save just as they did in the second World War.

That route, I think, is much more promising than any kind of compulsory saving feature. It does not, however, foreclose the possibility of working out more or less voluntary arrangements with workers to accept overtime in savings bonds or some kind of deferred expendable income. Some such techniques are perhaps worth exploring, especially if this defense program is going to go much higher, as many think it will, and defense workers are going to receive overtime pay without a commensurate increase in production (say a 30 per cent increase in take-home pay for 20 per cent more hours worked and less than 20 per cent more production).

On the other hand, I see nothing obnoxious about consumer credit controls as they now stand. I think it is easy to exaggerate both their effectiveness and their alleged burden on people with low incomes. The mere passage of time changes the picture. The consumer has only to save over a period of two, three, four, five months, or whatever it may be; with the passage of time he has saved enough to make the larger down payment required by the controls; and he is in the market again—perhaps too soon (though we do not have very good statistics) for the purpose of combating inflation. I believe that is the position of the Federal Reserve System.

In other words, I still feel that the monetary aspects of inflation constitute the critical area for action. The revolutionary character of the monetary experience through which we have passed has not yet fully sunk into the public consciousness. Money, bank credit, interest rates, and bank reserves are today being recognized by close students of the subject as sensitive instruments which are capable of governing the level of economic activity in a way that was not recognized by the Congress when it provided for wage and price controls in the DPA.

It is becoming progressively more obvious that a balanced budget and tight credit controls can indeed prevent inflation. The politicians and their Washington agents will continue for a time to parrot the phrase, "We need not only indirect monetary and fiscal measures but also direct controls over wages and prices." *If* we continue a tough credit policy and finance this war as we go, the politicians who hand us *that* story will look more and more foolish as time goes on.

To be sure, defense expenditure has built up more slowly than anticipated. Tax revenues have been better than was expected—due largely, however, to the credit inflation itself, which represents a poor way to keep a budget balanced. While there is talk of military expenditures' reaching a fifty billion dollar rate by the end of 1951, there is also reason to believe that this goal will not be attained. International tensions, in spite of surface phenomena, are declining, and the prospect of an early all-out war with the USSR is receding; indeed, many responsible people believe that it will not occur unless *we* provoke it. The 8.5 billion dollar foreign-aid program requested by the Administration will not be fully voted. The labor leaders' strike against the government after the Wage Stabilization Board announced its 10 per cent catching-up formula, as well as subsequent virtual refusal of the union representatives to make any sacrifice in this war effort by shouldering more taxes or foregoing any shrinkage in their living standards, is causing the Administration to spread the rearmament program over a longer period of time. This means a reduced "peaking up" of the defense expenditures. Thus the necessary shrinkage of the civilian economy is delayed and reduced.

The anticipatory buying since Korea, the balanced budget, and the tighter credit controls will reduce the inflationary pressures below what was anticipated some months ago. A further tax increase of five billion dollars may be required to keep the budget balanced. The latter half of 1951 is not likely to be a period of feverish expansion in most sectors of the economy. Steel, copper, and probably aluminum will remain tight or perhaps get even tighter. Under present Washington plans a number of nonferrous metals and some types of steel will have been put on a 100 per cent allocation basis by the beginning of 1952. Residential construction will continue to taper off. Partly because of credit controls and partly because of anticipatory buying and hoarding as well as scarcity of raw materials, durable goods production and buying are likely to remain at modest levels. Plant and equipment expansion, however, will go forward in large volume. Unfilled orders in the hands of manufacturers are very large—fifty-one billion dollars at the end of March 1951 as against twenty-two billion dollars a year earlier.

A while ago it was anticipated in Washington that the figure for wage and salary income would stand by December 1951 at twenty billion dollars to twenty-five billion above that of December 1950. Now it is generally believed that the increase will be considerably less. Commodity prices have shown a down-trend. One spot commodity index declined from 221 at the beginning of April 1951 to 210 by June 4, 1951. The futures index in the same period declined from 208 to 189.

Thus, while the picture is a mixed one, there is some reason to believe that inflationary pressures will not be so strong at the end of 1951 as they were a year previous. Yet we would be on dangerous ground if we projected the current lull into the future.

In the months ahead net profits are expected to continue to decline to pre-Korea levels or lower. Stiff price controls and rollbacks and "flexible" wage "stabilization" are intensifying the squeeze. Contract renegotiation and cutbacks in civilian production will take, for many companies, another chunk out of profits. The two corporate tax increases of 1950, along with the excess profits tax, applied to only part of the year's earnings. In 1951 these tax increases will apply to the full year, and another general corporate tax increase will be on the books before the autumn frosts. Slower military expenditures than were previously anticipated and tight credit conditions will make the economy less buoyant. All these forces will mean reduced profits.

In the short space of a few years we cannot transform our economy to double or triple a relatively modest defense budget without wrenching or without pain. The events since March 1951 have demonstrated, however, that we do have it within our power to make this change without substantial inflation. We had our spree in the first eight months after Korea because we lacked the wisdom or the courage to do what was obviously necessary on the monetary front. We have now snubbed the inflationary pressures largely by technical procedures and adjustments. Price and wage controls have had little to do with this change.

In the period ahead the pain of avoiding inflation, while the defense program expands, may be even more trying and testing than the pain of inflation. Were it not for the large number of people living on fixed and seriously lagging incomes, it would be easier for a democracy to finance such a program by permitting some inflation than it would be to prevent it.

Actually, we are likely to do a little better job of avoiding price increases in the period ahead than we did in the first eight months of the Korean war, but we are not likely to avoid a partial repetition of what we have experienced.

Let me conclude on a somewhat optimistic note. Is it not possible that we have completely misread the meaning of Korea? After all, Dean Acheson had considered Korea as being on the outside of our defense perimeter, and he gave Stalin, in a sense, a free and open hand; and then we double-crossed Stalin. In any event, there is room for doubt. I think it is not only very dangerous but unnecessary for us to get into the mood of thinking that we must continue indefinitely to put such a great burden on our economy. There is a limit to our capacity, whether it be the extent to which popular support will go or the degree of economic strain we can stand or some other factor. Just as in the case of life insurance, you can carry too much and break yourself. And in this case maybe our survival is not being so seriously threatened as some seem to think it is.

Granted the "Commies" want to conquer the world. But does not a careful study of these thoughts and writings show also that they have had a terrible inferiority complex in Moscow? They are badly frightened for their own security. So I think we are in real danger of misreading the Soviet Union too. That does not mean that I am for going back to pre-Korean defense expenditures, but I refuse to swallow whole the terrible things that are supposed to be in the Soviet blueprint for the near-term future. We are not weak and are less vulnerable than the alarmists would have us believe.

A Labor Point of View

I should like to start by explaining that I am not so complacent about the situation as some authorities, including Dr. Schmidt, seem to be, perhaps because I approach the problem of the defense program and inflation from a slightly different set of assumptions.

The present lull in the Korean war situation, and the accompanying relaxation of the consumer durable goods market and the price structure, it seems to me, should not encourage us to sit back and say, "Things are all well. Let's continue to pursue the same policy as we have in the past."

My initial assumption is that the Korean situation is the first of a series of unprovoked aggressions on the part of the Soviet Union and its satellite Iron Curtain countries. I am firmly convinced that the Soviet Union hopes eventually to engage in an all-out war, the early stages of which will be started during the next few years by actions of its satellite countries, in Iran, Yugoslavia, the Philippines, Formosa, and other areas of the world. I think that is the current view of the Administration in Washington.

If you start with that assumption, then you must ask, "What can we do in the way of programming to prevent the Soviet Union from carrying out its intentions to engage in an all-out war—which it appears at the moment to be planning to do?" Probably everyone is aware of the fact that the Soviet Union and the Kremlin and the Politburo could do no greater harm to America than to sit back and say, "For the next six months or year we will take no action. The American people will interpret that as peaceful intentions on our part and consequently there will be a letdown in their military and defense program. Then, six months or a year from now, we shall spring on them, and they won't be prepared, just as they weren't prepared in June of 1950 for the Korean situation."

We must build a strong military force for ourselves and our Allies abroad. Such a strong military force is the only way we can demonstrate physically to the Politburo and the Kremlin in Moscow that we mean business and that we will resist aggression as we resisted aggression in Korea. Perhaps, by building this force and being prepared for aggressive action on the part of the Soviets we can convince them that they ought not to start the third world war. I hope so.

In any event the assumption I start from requires that the military program, which began with expenditures at an annual rate of thirteen billion dollars a year ago, which at mid-1951 had reached an annual rate of thirty billion, and which it is contemplated will run at an annual rate of from fifty billion to fifty-five billion or even sixty-five billion by June 1952, is a program which we should all support and carry through. Such a program, which will double the mid-1951 rate of military expenditure and more than quadruple the rate of military expenditure of a year ago, requires that various kinds of positive steps be taken to protect our domestic economy.

First of all, we must have, as we now do, a program of allocation, priorities, controlled distribution of materials, and expansion of basic capacity—that is, an immediate and long-range program involving several different and specific types of action.

If the present situation continues as a semi-hot and not an all-out aggressive war, then we must expect to continue to maintain a strong military force involving large-scale military expenditures over a period of three, four, five, or more years.

To accomplish that goal over the long run, we must engage now in a program of expansion of productive capacity in basic industries, such as steel, aluminum, nonferrous metals, and copper.

Then, having reached the maximum level of military strength that we feel we must attain to resist the Soviet Union or prevent it from moving into a third all-out war, and having achieved a high level of production, we can meet the military requirements as well as the domestic requirements and begin to rebuild our domestic economy.

Even then, instead of curtailing production, we should continue to expand. In that way we can eventually go back to living a reasonably normal life at the same time that we maintain a strong military establishment to convince the Russians of the folly of starting a third world war.

During the interim period—while we are arriving at that eventual point, which may not be for three, four, or even five years—many dislocations will be taking place in our domestic economy. Production of automobiles, domestic appliances, aluminum ware, and so forth will necessarily have to be curtailed. And, as we curtail production of domestic goods, shifting from these areas to the military goods areas, we are bound to have dislocations in the economy which require CMP and all that goes with it in the way of planning, priorities, allocations, and programming requirements to meet the goals of military strength and expanded production.

Simultaneously, during this period of shifts in the use of materials, while we are building a military force and attempting to expand capacity, it is essential that we engage in a series of other economic measures to stabilize our economy.

At this point I would agree with Dr. Schmidt that the pay-as-you go objective is part of a sound and essential program. That assumes, however, that we have an equitable type of tax program. And I am afraid that Dr. Schmidt would not agree with me on what the tax program should be. But I do not want to go into that here. Suffice it to say that I object strenuously to resorting to the sales tax or any other kind of regressive taxation during this period.

Let me call your attention to the fact—as reported by the Federal Reserve Board—that in 1949 the five million family spending units making up the top 10 per cent in order of income received spent for consumer goods slightly in excess of the total amount spent by the twenty-five million family spending units making up the bottom 50 per cent. If we are going to tackle the problem of taxing where money is spent, we ought to tax at the high-income level as well as the low-income level.

A sales tax is, as we will all admit, a regressive tax, a tax that is in inverse proportion to income. Low-income people have to spend a greater proportion of their income for a sales tax than do high-income individuals. A sales tax of 2 per cent or 3 per cent, or whatever it might be, prevents the low-income individual from buying commodities, whereas an individual with an income, say, of $12,000 or more, makes less of a sacrifice and indeed can probably take care of the tax out of his surplus or accumulated savings. Therefore, I say a sales tax is inequitable.

I would support, rather, a general, over-all income tax rise similar to the 12½ per cent which the Ways and Means Committee has voted, as contrasted to an increase of 3 percentage points and then a sales tax to make up the difference. I think that move of the Ways and Means Committee is a step in the right direction. In other words, I think we can raise sufficient tax revenue to meet budget requirements by an adequate and sound tax structure along progressive lines. I consider it not a valid argument to say that we started with a highly progressive tax system and that regressive taxes therefore merely make the whole thing less progressive. I object to moving in that direction at all.

As for the question of monetary policy, again I do not agree with Dr. Schmidt for various reasons which I do not feel I should try to explain here. There may develop a very serious need for refunding much of the federal debt; refunding of present debt is obviously going to be at high rates during the coming year and the year after, to say nothing of what may be added to it in the way of a deficit if Congress is not successful in reducing nonessential expenditures. I am inclined to think that the monetary policy of the Federal Reserve Board in refusing to buy "Governments" will have to be relaxed, and that we cannot permit "Governments" to move to a very low rate, much below the 96 or 97 rate of par at which they now stand.

But in my mind, besides being involved and complicated, that is a totally different problem from our main concern. It is more to the point, and more serious, that Dr. Schmidt and other representatives of the Chamber of Commerce and National Association of Manufacturers are now claiming that a pay-as-you-go tax program and a monetary program of bank and consumer credit controls are sufficient to meet the inflationary pressures and to stabilize our domestic economy during this interim period. That just does not make sense to me.

We are trying to reach the ultimate goal of expansion of production, so we can support a military economy and a growing domestic economy at the same time; on that there is agreement. Certainly such a goal requires during the build-up stage, in addition to a strong tax program, direct control to stabilize prices and wages. And I frankly am at a loss to understand why the representatives of business in the United States have appeared before the Banking and Currency Committees of the Senate and House and demanded that price and wage stabilization not be included in the extension of the Defense Production Act.

One labor leader has charged—and maybe he is right—that big business in America is attempting to engage in a conspiracy with organized labor. It's almost as if big business were saying: "O.K., boys. Price and wage controls are not good. Let's remove them. We can do what we want with prices; you can do what you want with wages." But that is an irresponsible proposition, and labor will never accept it. For the fact is that, during this period when shortages will occur and distribution will be disturbed, we must, of necessity, have price and wage stabilization in addition to tax and monetary policy if inflation is to be held in check.

I wish I could say more about the wage stabilization program. I do not agree that it is not effective in Washington. I would say, on the contrary, that it is exceedingly effective. If we did not have it in effect as it is now operating, we would see much larger wage increases than we have seen. And, after all, nobody is proposing that we freeze wages. Nobody is proposing that we freeze prices either; certainly they are not being frozen under the margin-markup policies of OPS. But this does not mean that there should not be *some* effective means of price stabilization during the period.

As for voluntary bank credit restraints, would anybody think of saying to the trade unions of the United States: "You control your own wages; we have confidence that you will be able to stop wage increases?" Nobody would ever conceive of suggesting that to the trade unions, and I would not suggest it because it obviously would not work. But the Federal Reserve Board has said to the banks of the country, "You control credit. You stop inflationary credit through the voluntary system of bank credit loans which you now have." In my opinion that is not a sufficient credit policy on the part of our government.

We should have authority, such as does not now exist, to increase reserve requirements or create special reserve accounts over and above the present limitations on reserve requirements of banks. We should have more direct control of bank credit. When we talk about fiscal policy and monetary and credit policy, therefore, let us not talk about the voluntary bank credit policy we now have, but let us talk about a more effective policy which would control the bank credits of the country in a much more equitable way. These measures are all essential parts of any over-all program.

As for consumer credit controls, I agree that we have to have them, but I am a bit disturbed by the fact that Regulations X and W as they now operate discriminate against the individual in the lower income bracket. As a matter of fact, they ration commodities or housing according to the ability to buy and not according to need. Obviously, people must sacrifice during a defense period, and the low-income persons, who constitute the majority of the people in America, must also sacrifice. But when, for example, the individual who has a one-third down payment to put on a car can buy it while an individual who does not have the one-third down payment cannot, that is inequitable and unfair in a credit policy. Therefore, our credit policy—and this applies particularly to housing—should be reoriented so as to permit the limited supply of goods which consumer credit attempts to allocate through credit sources to be properly and equitably distributed to consumers as a whole.

In other words, I think Regulations W and X should be continued, but with revisions. If an individual can really show that he cannot make the larger down payment required by the regulations, if the commodity is available and is essential to him—suppose again, it is an automobile, a used car, or a new car, and he produces evidence that it is essential to his work—then he ought to be permitted somehow to get a relaxation of Regulation W so that he can buy it. A car these days is not a luxury, as we all know, but a very definite necessity, particularly if workers are going to be transferring from one plant to another—from civilian to military goods plants.

As far as that is concerned, so long as television sets and radio sets are glutting the market, as they are now, I think it is wise that in their case the regulation should at least be relaxed to the extent that —as in the case of automobiles—the trade-in value be considered as part of the down payment itself rather than as a reduction in the sales price.

As for Regulation X, I think the whole orientation, with the size of the down payment increasing at an extremely progressive rate as the price of the house increases, is a good one. But I am disturbed that the housing program does not permit the construction of houses for those people who need them; that the people who really need them cannot buy them. There are, for example, many individuals moving into defense areas where there is no housing available for them.

Housing is an essential part of defense production. A recent estimate of an auto company—if I recall correctly—indicated that in one of their plants during the course of the last year or so they added fourteen hundred workers, and six hundred left in a period of six months, giving the definite reason that they could not find housing for their families.

The housing program ought to be revised to permit more construction for such workers as against the construction of other kinds of houses (for instance, those selling for $35,000 and more); and, where workers need houses and can prove the necessity, the size of the required down payments ought to be reduced. A 10 per cent down payment may not sound like much; but on a $10,000 house, it is $1,000, and that may be way beyond the means of a defense worker moving into a new locality.

Now let me go on to comment on the thought that extra pay for overtime work is inflationary. The suggestion has even been made in some quarters that if all workers put in forty-eight hours of work each week and only got paid for forty, that would help to control inflation. In the first place, obviously, the increased income resulting from overtime payment is income and *does* create demand and to that extent *is* inflationary. However, we must not lose sight of the fact that, for every increased hour of overtime work, increased products are being turned out, though of course many of them are military and therefore do not add to the supply of domestic items available to consumers. The significant point is that the level of production is being raised through the overtime payment incentive.

Remember, too, that the corporations are getting a profit from the increased production and the increased sale of these items. The fact is that the move from a forty-hour week to a forty-eight-hour week spreads overhead costs over a greater number of units of output, which—according to a Department of Labor study—about balances out the increased wage bill resulting from overtime payment. I would say that if corporations would agree not to take any increased profit from increased production during the overtime period, unions and workers would also agree to sacrifice and not take the increased overtime payment. However, I think it is un-American to deny corporations the profits they would derive from this kind of operation, and equally un-American to deprive workers of the money they would receive as overtime payments.

Of course this is much more than an economic problem. We are dealing with tradition, with legislative enactment, with trade union background and worker experience. Let me remark that the National Labor Management Manpower Policy Committee in Washington, on which I have been sitting as a member, had a statement up before it for consideration which was unanimously adopted by the Inter-Agency Manpower Policy Committee, and that policy sets forth the need for maintaining the provisions of the Fair Labor Standards and Walsh-Healy Acts that require overtime payments. Certainly it is not beside the point to call attention to the fact that the whole problem of labor morale is tied to this basic issue of overtime.

A lot more could be said on the problem of overtime. For the purposes of the present discussion, however, two observations will suffice: (1) The redistribution of overhead costs per unit of output keeps overtime payments from being a cost factor in inflation; (2) As for their being an income factor in inflation, the same basic argument applies here as in the case of productivity and cost of living: it is not the receipt of income but its expenditure which is basically inflationary, and that is where we ought to direct our greatest efforts.

I would suggest, in conclusion, that we do proceed on a pay-as-you-go basis, but that the tax policy implementing it be fairer and more equitable, based upon ability to pay and equality of sacrifice—if those two terms mean much. It should be accompanied by (1) a credit policy involving larger reserve requirements and compulsory restraint of bank credits; (2) a reoriented consumer credit program; and (3) a price and wage stabilization program which holds the levels of prices and wages. Further, during the period when these kinds of controls are in force, we should engage in a long-range program of expansion of capacity in our basic industries in the hope that four or five years from now productive capacity will be sufficient to meet both our military and our domestic requirements, and that then—but not before then—we can remove direct controls.

I think it is essential to keep in mind that the argument which is frequently made that we have a free, democratic government in America, and hence we ought not to engage in direct controls, is just propaganda, not sound reasoning. Nobody likes controls; nobody wants controls. But I would much rather see controls in existence for a two-year or three-year or four-year period while we are adjusting to this new situation, involving, as it does, a high level of military expenditures, than not see controls and have runaway inflation.

An Economist's Point of View

The thing which distresses me most about modern controversy is not that people are given labels for their *interpretation* of the facts. What is really upsetting is that they are increasingly labeled merely for *stating* the facts. Our impatient and romantic democracy seems to feel that the man who states the (to his audience) unwelcome facts has somehow personally *created* those facts; and that by shutting up or getting rid of the *man* you also get rid of the *problem*. If the room is cold, smash the thermometer!

What is the duty of the economist in such an atmosphere? The truth and the *whole* truth. A man cannot control the shifting sands of party maneuvering. But he can control his own scientific integrity. Believing with all my soul that intelligent policy cannot be framed without recognizing *all* the facts, believing that it is my scientific duty to hedge on none of them, however distasteful, I am trying, in my work, to give the truth as I see it so that, whatever the event, I hope to be able to say that I tried to do my part.

Surely everyone can see that the distressing necessities entailed in any real effort to curb inflation—necessities which an honest man cannot gloss over—are no creation of mine or of any other economist. They are rooted in the nature of war itself. As a Southerner and a Georgian, I am personally and acutely aware of the truth of General Sherman's brief epitome: "War is Hell." There it is. The whole thing. We only get ourselves in greater trouble by trying to make it out a battle of rose leaves.

Clearly the inflationary problem depends largely upon the diplomatic and military one. And to read the future in diplomacy and war one needs a clairvoyant, not an economist. It is also clear that by some short-sighted program of appeasement or disarmament we could avoid the inflationary pressure. Such a policy, I think, would be disastrous.

Let us assume that world conditions will continue to keep us in a tense productive situation and see what some of the problems are which this situation involves. I will briefly summarize the general problem and then discuss two subordinate points: (1) the notion that inflation "creates savings" and "balances the budget"; (2) the idea that money wages, even in wartime, should rise in accordance with "productivity" or to "maintain the standard of living."

The essence of the war-inflation problem can be very briefly given. It has two sides: technical and monetary. On the technical side the problem is to get as great an output of war goods as possible. During the last war we began with an immense reservoir of unemployed, so that it was possible to pile a great war effort on top of a given civilian output with relatively little difficulty and relatively small sacrifice. But today no comparable slack exists. In order to increase output we must, among other things, reduce the consumption level!

This brings us to the second half of the problem—the monetary one. People often talk as if all that was needed to prevent inflation was to balance the budget. Unfortunately, much more is implied. Neither the monetary nor the technical problem can be solved unless we somehow *cut down on people's spending*. Even if the government budget is balanced through taxes, people may still be able to borrow from the banks, cut in on savings, and so on, and thus keep on spending. The result is that prices will keep on going up, barring controls, and even *with* controls the history of the Nazis shows that the most terrific political power cannot prevent a black market if money is increased indefinitely. The financial job, therefore, if we are to get the needed war output *and* to prevent inflation, is to collect enough money from the right people really to reduce the demand for civilian goods. We need to go at this two ways: (1) by making bank credit less available and (2) by increasing taxes on the lower income groups, who do the great bulk of the consuming.

Inflation cannot possibly do this job for us—that is, if we expect (as many people seem to) that we can have just a "little" inflation to "balance the budget" and then stop. The trouble is that while inflation may raise money income and thus increase the yield of the taxes, *it also increases the price of everything.* So when the government goes to spend its money, the money will not buy *as many* war goods as before. Therefore a *bigger* appropriation will be needed next time; that in turn will unbalance the budget again, which will call for a "little" more inflation, and so the spiral goes on. Once more, of course, price control will help *if mass consumption is not being increased.* But if money wages are being pushed up and spending again encouraged, the black market and general collapse of enforcement will again be risked.

Let us get the point clear. The problem is that spending *must* be reduced. The enormous bulk of the spending is done in the lower income groups. We cannot therefore charge the war to the rich. They may have more money and spend more money, but there just are not enough of them. The only question is: Shall we reduce mass consumption through inflation or taxation? For *reduce* consumption in any case we must.

Discussions of the tax burden in the sense of possible "limits" beyond which we "cannot" go seem to me largely irrelevant now. This is a war of survival! We have to get armed quickly and stay armed. We, to be sure, have the choice between good and bad taxes. We have the choice between imposing the burden through inflation or imposing it through taxation. But whatever the method, the burden must somehow be imposed.

We are now right where England was at the time of Munich. It is obvious that we may get another Munich. But do not ever fall for the notion that any possible understanding can be reached with a Leninist, Marxist country. There is absolutely nothing that we could do that would induce the Soviet Union not to attack us as soon as she felt ready to do so. Anybody who thinks there can be an understanding with a Leninist, Marxist country has never bothered to study Communism. All you need to do is to read Lenin's *The State and Revolution.*

I often think that the best way to deceive people is to print your most secret thoughts in a book and publish it. Nobody will take you seriously. Nobody took Napoleon seriously when he discussed his metaphysical plans for the unification of Europe. Nobody took what Hitler said in *Mein Kampf* seriously; all that was academic nonsense. And look what Napoleon and Hitler did! In the same way, we may be tempted not to take Lenin and Stalin seriously. But certainly it is safer to think that they too are deadly serious. As for their being frightened for their own security, as Dr. Schmidt said, it is simply good psychology to figure that the "scareder" they are, the sooner they may jump us.

I turn now to another argument which may have disastrous consequences for the anti-inflationary program. That is the argument that wages should go up even in wartime "to keep pace with productivity." This argument is greatly overused even in peacetime.

Last May I attended a symposium on the labor problem held at the American University, Washington, D. C. We discussed at that session the normal amount by which wages in peacetime might go up with productivity without risking inflation. Professor John Maurice Clark, making every possible allowance, figured that average money wages even in peacetime could not safely rise more than about 3½ per cent a year.

I had the honor of editing that symposium, and it has just been published under the title of *The Impact of the Union.*[8] I should like to quote from the remarks of two liberal economists who can by no stretch of the imagination be called anti-union, Professor Boulding of Michigan and Professor Samuelson of Massachusetts Institute of Technology.

Professor Samuelson said, "Labor leaders as a whole are kidding

[8] New York, Harcourt, Brace and Company, 1951.

themselves and they know it if they think they can get 10 per cent money increases all around per annum, which will eventually result in 10 per cent real-wage increases per annum all around."

Professor Boulding summarized the discussion in the following jingle:

We all (or nearly all) consent
If wages rise by ten per cent
It puts a choice before the nation
Of unemployment or inflation.

But these figures are pre-Korea! Think how much more applicable they are now. For the whole point is that even if productivity does rise now, it will be productivity *in war goods.* The only justification for productivity wage increases in peacetime is that they accompany increase in the supply of civilian goods. But in wartime there is nothing more for civilians to buy. The productivity argument is thus almost wholly bogus.

Equally so is the standard-of-living argument. As I have shown, the standard of living *must* fall to permit increased war output. But if we try to raise wages every time prices rise, we only make the job harder. We are committing ourselves to an impossible goal.

Unionists today seek to evade these arguments by whipping up feeling about "profiteers," and I should like to conclude by quoting from another unimpeachably liberal source, John Maynard Keynes:

> Lenin is said to have declared that the best way to destroy the Capitalist System was to debauch the currency. By a continuing process of inflation, Governments can confiscate, secretly and unobserved, an important part of the wealth of their citizens . . . the Governments of Europe, being many of them at this moment reckless in their methods as well as weak, seek to direct on to a class known as "profiteers" the popular indignation against the more obvious consequences of their vicious methods. These "profiteers" are, broadly speaking, the entrepreneur class of capitalists, that is to say, the active and constructive element in the whole capitalist society. . . . By directing hatred against this class, therefore, the European Governments are carrying a step further the fatal process which the subtle mind of Lenin had consciously conceived. *The profiteers are a consequence and not a cause of rising prices.*[4]

[4] *Essays in Persuasion,* p. 77.

PRICE AND WAGE CONTROLS

Thomas L. Karsten, J. Keith Mann, and Harold J. Walter

Price Control Policy

Many businessmen today question whether there actually is a need for continuing controls. Controls are always very onerous to work with. They make a businessman's life considerably more difficult; and therefore, when businessmen can look about and see soft markets in many areas, not to mention a more extreme expression of a downward trend like the Macy-Gimbel's price war, they say to themselves, "Why am I continuing to be troubled by these very complicated and onerous regulations?"

I think the answer to that must be found in a comparison of the situation as we know it today with the situation as we experienced it yesterday. We found in the first half of 1950, even before the Korean outbreak, that we were already in a semi-inflationary situation. The inventory recession of 1948 and 1949 had already been replaced in the first half of 1950 with a considerable inventory build-up, and an increase in employment of some four and a half million had already taken place. The rate of business expansion, along with bank loans, was increasing considerably, with the result that wholesale prices between January and June of 1950 rose some 4 per cent, and the consumer price index climbed 2 per cent.

This fairly mild kind of inflationary process was intensified, as we now know only too well, by the shots that were fired in Korea. It is interesting to examine what happened as a result of that Korean outbreak and what the economic situation actually was during the latter half of 1950 when we saw prices escalate so seriously.

NOTE: Mr. Karsten is Director of the Consumer Soft Goods Division of the Office of Price Stabilization; Mr. Mann is Vice-Chairman, Review and Appeals Committee, Wage Stabilization Board; Mr. Walter is President, Bachmann-Uxbridge Worsted Corporation.

Mr. Karsten discusses price control, and Mr. Mann, wage stabilization; Mr. Walter provides a case study from the woolen and worsted business.

Government expenditure during the half year following the Korean outbreak was not much greater than it had been during the first half of the previous year. It was at the rate of about three billion dollars per month and, actually, was not deficit spending. Indeed, there was a surplus of around 170 million dollars. The rate of government expenditure could not alone account for this price spiral. Nor did business expansion increase perceptibly in the latter half of 1950 over the early half of 1950; nor, for that matter, did credit expansion or bank loans.

Consumer spending, however, increased some 5 per cent, and that was translated into a 13 per cent increase in inventory build-up. It was this "scare buying" (I think we can call it that) at almost every level of the economy which caused prices to skyrocket as they did, encouraged also to some extent by business expansion, the increase in bank loans, and the expansion of credit that was taking place through that same period. The net result in terms of price increases was that from June 1950 to January 1951 wholesale prices rose 23 per cent, and the consumer price index rose 11 per cent.

The Office of Price Stabilization, somewhat belatedly, stepped into the picture. I say belatedly because that is exactly what I think it was. On the other hand, perhaps one of the advantages of living in a democracy is that an administration, whether it be Republican or Democratic, views with some apprehension the imposition of controls such as price and wage controls and materials allocations, and adopts them only after a good deal of soul searching and backing-and-filling. And so these controls were not imposed until a considerable period of time had elapsed.

As far as price control was concerned, we began by issuing the General Ceiling Price Regulation (GCPR). That regulation provided that all prices were frozen at their highest level in the period December 19, 1948, to January 25, 1949. We immediately began following up that regulation with the issuance of what we have termed interim general regulations designed to bring large groups of producers and sellers out from under GCPR because we recognized that GCPR, left as it was without immediate change, would considerably impede normal business activity. We therefore had to get out regulations which would more naturally fit the constantly changing atmosphere of business enterprise. Many of those interim regulations have now been issued, and manufacturers and sellers are working under them.

The result of our having begun the control of prices was translated quite rapidly into the Consumer Price Index and the Wholesale Price Index. Thus we find that from January to March 1951 wholesale prices went up only 4 per cent and the Consumer Price Index only 3 per cent. In the period from March to June 1951 wholesale prices actually fell off by 2 per cent, while the Consumer Price Index remained stable and even promised some decrease.

We have, however, a situation which is still fraught with the danger of a high degree of inflationary pressure. Government expenditures, which through March 1951 remained at a level of some three billion dollars per month, increased in the next three months to a level of approximately five billion dollars per month, and are expected to increase to some six billion per month through the fiscal year 1952.

Inventories, which had gone up about eleven billion in the fourth quarter of 1950, increased only seven billion in the first quarter of 1951; the rate of increase of inventory, while 22 per cent over pre-Korea as of March 1951, must be compared with unfilled orders which as of that same date are 118 per cent above pre-Korea. It is estimated that, given the present rate of government expenditure, we are going to have a deficit of some sixteen billion dollars in 1952.

Now, taking into consideration this level of government expenditure, the estimated deficit, the declining rate of inventory build-up, and the increases in purchasing power which is building up daily because of the increases in employment and in wages, we have to conclude that there is a much more serious situation inflationwise than ever existed in 1950. The pressures today are *real* pressures. They are not merely the pressures of scare buying as was the case during the 1950 period. Therefore, it would be extremely unwise to relax controls at a time like this when we recognize the existence of such pressures.

There are, however, a considerable number of people, representing a substantial body of opinion, who claim that direct controls like price controls are not necessary and that their function can be accomplished by indirect controls. This raises several distinct problems.

First, there is the problem of whether indirect controls can actually be expected to sop up excess purchasing power. If we anticipate a deficit of some sixteen billion dollars, we must anticipate the necessity for an additional tax levy of some nineteen billion to twenty billion to sop up all the excess purchasing power there would be. Thus far, at any rate, Congress seems to have decided on a tax increase of around seven billion dollars at the most. If it were to impose a nineteen billion or a twenty billion levy, I think the result would be a stifling of production and a curtailment of industrial expansion when we need them most.

As for credit controls, which are the counterpart of high tax levies and also operate indirectly, I think we would find there too that any very serious restrictions would have an unfortunate effect upon business expansion and sales volume.

The question has also been raised whether direct controls will not merely repress inflation rather than cure it. It is true that direct controls, such as price controls, in and of themselves do not cure inflation. Furthermore, when price controls are used to "keep the lid on" artificially, a much greater inflationary rise is likely to occur at the time of their subsequent removal than if they had never been used at all. Therefore, it is better to use direct controls *plus* indirect controls, such as tax and credit controls. Together they can succeed quite admirably in controlling an inflationary situation in terms of keeping the lid on prices *and* reducing the pressures resulting from a high level of consumer income and government spending.

There is the additional question whether price controls do not actually stifle production. On this point we have the experience of the OPA in the second World War to guide us, although admittedly the analogy between the present and the period of the OPA is not exact.

In any event, we found under OPA that production in general

went up as much as 191 per cent over 1940, notwithstanding price controls; the production of manufactured goods, 295 per cent; the production of durable goods, 245 per cent; and the production of textiles, even though admittedly disappointing, some 134 per cent. By contrast, during the period of decontrol the rate of increase in production was but one-fifth of what it had been during the period of control.

So, there is reason to believe that, at least in the short run, price controls are not likely to decrease production appreciably. It is only when they are kept on over a very considerable period of time that they might have a depressive effect upon production. That, I admit, is a danger, though we cannot be positive about it.

Take the matter of beef, which is still a sore subject around OPS. I almost wince when I hear the word. The threatened beef scarcity —the one we were supposed to have if the rollbacks of beef prices were not removed—was exactly that, a threat. Cattlemen may hold cattle on the range because they feel that by creating a shortage at the market level they can generate sufficient pressures to blow the lid off beef prices. We have attempted to roll back the price of beef, as you know, and the cattlemen do not like that. I can understand how they feel. But thus far, at any rate, there has been no proof that price control has resulted in any decrease in cattle production.

The cattlemen have claimed that they could not produce at a sufficient profit under the ceilings we imposed. We are not at all convinced of their case, though they have had a considerable opportunity to express their views both before our agency and before Congressional committees and other groups in Washington. In plain words, convincing facts have not been submitted indicating that the ceilings we imposed were below the level they require to produce at a considerable profit.

This beef situation, incidentally, is a good case in point in connection with the argument which is made that if you only have enough production, you do not need price control, regardless of what the other factors in the economy may be. Beef production has increased very substantially since mid-1950. Nonetheless, beef prices have gone up faster and higher than the prices of almost any other domestically produced item.

The matter of profit control is one which businessmen bring up very frequently when they talk about price control. In this respect a great deal of misapprehension has been created generally by Eric Johnston's letter, in which, writing to Mr. DiSalle, he stated that with the end of the interim period of price control an industry earning standard of somewhere in the neighborhood of 85 per cent of the best three years of 1946–1949 should govern the adjustment of price ceilings with respect to particular industries.

What that letter purported to say was that *in a situation where a particular company or segment of an industry finds that the application of the pricing standard established for the industry decreases its profits below the level of 85 per cent of the best three years in the period 1946 to 1949,* then it has the right to come in and ask for an increase in its prices. The statement applies only to that specific situation.

When we establish a pricing standard for an industry, we do it on the basis of what is generally conceived to be fair and equitable, quite without reference to this 85 per cent earning standard. The 85 per cent standard is to take care of hardship cases. To put it another way, this so-called 85 per cent standard is more a guarantee of equity than a ceiling limiting the profit that an industry may enjoy under a pricing standard developed by us.

Let me illustrate. Suppose the volume of sales in an industry is expanding to double the pre-Korea volume. Will profits be allowed to double, or will they be held to the level of the previous year's profits? In this case, assuming the existence of a regulation governing the industry which is such as to enable the industry to expand to this extent and to increase its profits to this extent, obviously there would be no necessity for the industry to apply for an adjustment and to seek the application of that 85 per cent standard, because it would not be in a hardship situation. It would be, as a matter of fact, in a very favorable situation. So long as we were *generally* satisfied with the level of prices in that particular industry or for that particular group of commodities which the industry was producing, we would not be interested in looking into the matter of whether it was making "X" dollars or "Y" dollars—85 per cent of the three best years of 1946–1949, or 100 per cent, or 115 per cent.

In some instances a certain amount of cutback of production can be carried by an industry without its being placed in a hardship situation. If, however, we find cases in which industries are in a hardship situation as a result of a cutback in production due, for example, to NPA allocations of materials, we would have to give price relief according to such standards as will be developed to meet that kind of a situation.

Any substantial increase in wages will have to be reflected to some extent in prices. We cannot set price ceilings without regard to what the manufacturer or producer or distributor encounters in the way of wage increases or materials cost increases, as the case may be. The regulations of an interim nature which we issued did of course permit a manufacturer to add to his pre-Korean prices such increases in labor costs as he may have experienced from the base period to March 15, 1951. If, as time goes on, wage increases result in still higher labor costs to these manufacturers, we shall have to review the formula that we have used thus far and make such adjustments as seem to be required in the interests of fairness to the producer. Cost increases up to July 26, 1951, are now allowed.

Another kind of question is also raised: Why did we impose such a burden on retailers, particularly small retailers, in figuring their prices? Let me say right away that what we did, I am convinced, helped the retailers in the end. A straight freeze of prices as of any given date is very inequitable—it penalizes some retailers and ensures windfalls for others—and there are too many retailers selling too many commodities for us to deal administratively with all the exceptions and still be fair. The use of "historical margins" is the only sound solution, since it allows the retailer's regular ways of doing business to determine his price ceilings—neither more nor less margin per item than before.

Of course, the onerous part—not for the big retailers with their careful records systems, but for the small ones who are the bulk of the retailers in the country—was the job of making up their price charts. We provided that the list date would be a date almost contemporary with the issuance of the order rather than back in October, November, or December 1950, though that would have been desirable if it could have been done. But most small retailers would not have known what they had in their stores on any such past date, and they certainly would not have known what their margins were.

So we had to say to them: "As of a particular date take an inventory of everything you have in your store; put down on a chart the relationship between cost and price of every one of those items; that is your margin with respect to each of those items, and you are frozen at that margin." That is precisely what we did. Actually CPR7 is not a difficult regulation to interpret, though it does require a certain amount of reading.

Most small retailers perhaps resisted the idea of taking an inventory because it is a lot of work. But once they got over the hump of taking the inventory, they were generally happier for having taken it, if only because for the first time in their lives they knew what they had in their stores and they knew the cost-price relationship of all their stock.

CPR7 is not just a nuisance. It is a device that comes as close as anything can to enabling a retailer to operate as he has always operated (subject of course to keeping his margins at the level of the particular date set by the regulation).

Perhaps a good note on which to conclude is to say something about the happy day when we can think of doing without controls once more. But that day may not be very close. The end of the Korean conflict does not automatically assure the end of inflationary pressures. We shall have to await the end of inflationary pressures, which means a decrease in government expenditure for armament and in allocation of materials for those purposes and a leveling off of the projected increase in consumer spending power.

When that time comes, we should, of course, actively begin the decontrol of those areas of the economy which are under price control. Even so, we could hardly take off all controls simultaneously without doing considerable injustice to the economy. It would have to be done progressively. Decontrolling took some time in OPA days, and I would assume that we would have to be equally careful, if not more so, this time.

In any event, no matter what else I may have accomplished, I hope I have made it clear that in OPS we have a very considerable regard for our responsibilities toward the business community. We do not feel that we are there to get in the way of the business community, but rather to handle its problems as expeditiously as we can, given the necessity for price control. We attempt to arrive at standards which are fair and equitable to all, and we attempt to give relief as quickly as may be possible in situations which warrant it. I think it can honestly be said that we are not theorists; that we are, rather, mostly people out of industry who have had a background that gives us cause to feel a real sense of responsibility about the job that we have been charged with accomplishing.

Wage Stabilization Policy

Let me begin by discussing the role of wage controls in an over-all program.[1] Mr. Karsten has already indicated that direct controls are a limited tool. The Wage Stabilization Board has recognized that fact from as far back as December 1950 when it suggested that measures to increase production by better use of our physical facilities and man power and measures to minimize the volume of money and credit in circulation were fundamental matters which had to be taken care of before direct controls on wages and prices, rent, real estate, credit, and so forth, could perform their function adequately.

Moreover, wage controls cannot do the whole job even of *wage* stabilization. During a period of mobilization such as we are now engaged in, more people are brought into the work force; they work longer hours; they move to higher paying industries. In some instances we have to attract them. We need incentives to production —and the money, the purchasing power, which is aggregated by mobilization is going to be greater. All we try to do is to stabilize

[1] The author gratefully acknowledges his debt to Dr. George W. Taylor, Chairman, Wage Stabilization Board, for the development, during the formative period of the Board's operations, of many of the thoughts expressed here.

the *rates,* not the *total amount* of money which goes into all the pay checks.

I realize that when people make more money, there is more demand for goods that are in short supply. But the wage structure in the United States is so complex and there are so many people working under different conditions that it is just impossible to devise an administratively workable policy which would, as far as wage controls are concerned, limit the total amount of money people could earn through working overtime or keep them from going into a higher paid industry or prohibit an industry which is essential from the mobilization point of view from attracting workers at a rate which upsets the local area situation.

We have the latter situation at the new atomic energy plant in South Carolina. The potential employees there are not industrial workers; they have to be attracted from all areas of the South. We simply have to permit the establishment of a wage level in that plant which is distinctly above the prevailing area rate, even though it is our usual policy in the case of new plants to approve only those rates which are (on the basis of submitted schedules and our own investigation) in line with other rates in the industry in the area. In other words, we must rely on taxation to drain off the extra purchasing power created by such additions to the total take-home pay of workers.

At the same time, wage controls do serve very useful purposes. For one thing, they can minimize competitive bidding for labor when labor markets are tight. If there is no control over this kind of thing, a factory on one side of the street will raise its rates to keep its workers or to attract workers; the fellow on the other side of the street will immediately raise his; the wage process begins spiraling. That we want to stop.

Secondly, controls can maintain normal wage and salary relationships. This is important to production; it is important to national morale. Some of the strikes we had during the second World War were over the simple question of normal relationships getting out of balance. Everyone has heard the story of the foreman who found himself earning less than the workers under him.

Thirdly, wage controls can do something to buttress Mr. Karsten's job of price control. Not only can prices be pushed up by runaway demand, but they can be pushed up by cost, and wages constitute about 53 per cent of the costs in manufacturing.

With that introduction, I would like to review some of the steps the Wage Stabilization Board has taken in order to stabilize the wage and salary level. Let me start with January 1951. Mr. Karsten has already gone over the general situation as of that time, and I shall simply point up the relevant wage aspects. In the last quarter of 1950, employers were granting wage increases to their workers to match rises in the cost of living or in anticipation of rises in the cost of living or to meet a present or anticipated man power problem. (When contracts were not reopenable, the old rates, of course, continued.) Some companies or industries were depressed; others were prosperous. The result was that when the freeze came on January 25, the normal wage structure was all out of balance because of the runaway which had been taking place.

The freeze was not intended as a permanent measure. It was merely supposed to give the government time to get an adequate control program under way.

The first major step which the Wage Stabilization Board took was the development of the so-called "catch-up formula." This is our General Regulation 6, which enables employers and employees to increase general wage and salary levels up to 10 per cent over those existing on January 15, 1950, without the prior approval of the Board. The 10 per cent figure—and it will be recalled that there was a dramatic fight over it in the Board—corresponded to representative wage settlements that had been reached by management and labor after the Korean outbreak. The majority of the settlements at that time clustered around 8 per cent. The Consumers' Price Index had risen slightly less than 8 per cent from the period January 1950 to January 1951. Consequently, the 10 per cent formula was sufficient to preserve the real value of the wage rate and at the same time was a means by which the various wage and salary elements could be restored to their relative pre-Korea positions.

When the Board issued this formula, it indicated its intention to review it in the light of the April 15, 1951, index figures. Regulation 6 was not envisaged as a final expression of wage policy, but, unfortunately, the 10 per cent amount became a magic figure in the public's mind.

The central theme of Regulation 6 was the equity of preserving the standard of living as it existed for workers in January 1950. This method of relating wages to the cost of living is a substantially similar approach to that taken during the second World War. Then wages up to 15 per cent above January 1941 levels were allowed under what was called the Little Steel Formula. The War Labor Board held that the cost of living was sufficiently stabilized during the war so that this basic policy, as set forth in the Little Steel Formula, could be adhered to; and during the latter part of the second World War we broke the relationship between wages and the cost of living.

When wage rates are related to the cost of living, the choice of a base date is a crucial decision. The fact that January 1941 was selected as the base in the second World War meant that employees had to forego the preservation of a higher hourly rate which they had achieved in free collective bargaining during 1941. But because there was a global war, because the allocation of our resources to the war effort was then about 50 per cent, the sacrifice seemed justified. Regulation 6, based on January 15, 1950, is likewise designed to assure a certain standard of living for workers.

It is important to recognize that today we have three million to four million employees covered by escalator clauses relating wages to the cost of living under some kind of formula. (This was not the case in the second World War. At that time there were relatively few escalator agreements, and one of the general orders of the War Labor Board after the adoption of the Little Steel Formula outlawed the operation of escalator agreements that went above the then 15 per cent formula.) Employers and unions in their free collective bargaining have increasingly sought a means of maintaining real wages for the duration of their contracts. Why? Because, apparently, collective bargaining has matured in our country, and the tendency is for long-term agreements, yet there is a lack of confidence in the stability of our cost of living. The utilization of these escalator clauses is one device for insuring the stability of long-term contracts through flexible adjustment of wage rates to changing conditions. Another way to achieve the same purpose, preferred by many, is to write a reopening clause into the contract in one form or another to provide for "certain uncertainty."

The Board broke up, it will be recalled, in February 1951, and for a time its activities were suspended. During this period Mr. Eric Johnston, the Economic Stabilization Administrator, issued a regulation authorizing the operation of escalator clauses negotiated prior to the freeze date. By its specific terms, the 10 per cent limit provided in the Board's Regulation 6 was made inapplicable when the escalation provided for a greater increase.

In some instances, of course, increases under escalator clauses exceeded our 10 per cent formula because general increases obtained in 1950 ran ahead of the rise in the cost of living between January 1950 and the date of the increase. The base date for computing this higher real wage was usually the date on which the contract was negotiated, and thus later than January 15, 1950. Workers covered by contracts containing escalator clauses were thus afforded more generous treatment than workers who were allowed to adjust their wages only under a formula choosing January 15, 1950, as a base date. I think it is apparent to everybody that there is at least some degree of conflict between Regulations 6 and 8; I doubt if many people would support the position that such a situation should be maintained over a long period.

Then the meat packing case came before the Board. The packing industry had a contract dated August 1950, which contained a reopening clause rather than an escalator clause. When the industry had reopened the contract, it had negotiated a wage which roughly corresponded to the change in the cost of living since the contract date.

When that case was presented, the question was whether it was equitable to allow the preservation of a higher standard of living for employees working under an escalator provision, but not for those who had chosen the future protection of a wage reopening clause. This is the kind of question which must be resolved in working out a wage stabilization policy.

In its decision in the meat packing case, the Board took the position that on the merits of the particular case it would be inequitable to use the January 15, 1950, base date to measure the cost of living adjustment and that the adjustment should be measured from the date of the labor agreement. It is my opinion that that is a sensible answer. I do not think the Wage Stabilization Board should follow a policy which would force management and unions into escalator-clause negotiations. But unless we provide for reopening clauses which permit the worker to get comparable benefits and thus maintain a minimum of freedom for management and labor, we will do just that.

On the other hand, I see no real reason for industry to stay away from escalator claims if it wants them. They are not *inevitably* inflationary. If one assumes some kind of stabilization in the cost of living, then the Consumers' Price Index of the Bureau of Labor Statistics or whatever other formula on which escalation is based does not rise, and the wages remain constant. Moreover, escalator clauses work both ways. If the cost of living goes down, the workers take a decrease, as was the case several times under the General Motors contract.

Of course, if the 10 per cent formula of Regulation 6 is effectively pierced through escalator and reopening clauses to the advantage of organized labor, provision will have to be made for allowing unorganized and white-collar salaries generally to move upward at the same time and to the same extent. But remember that such a provision would not *automatically* move them up; it simply is an economic fact, at this time or any time, that such salaries usually lag behind. The WSB does not set wages or salaries. It acts upon agreements reached between unions and management or on requests by employers to grant increases to their white-collar employees. In the latter case, the employers must take the initiative and ask for approval of the increases.

If the relation between wage rates and the cost of living is to follow the policy of either the second World War or of Regulation 6, it must be recognized that the real wage negotiated by many workers in their last freely negotiated contract would not be approved.

Congress, recalling the situation during the second World War when we first had price controls and then wage controls with no direct coördination of policy between the two, enacted into the present Defense Production Act a provision for one agency, with the Office of Price Stabilization and the Wage Stabilization Board under one man, the Economic Stabilization Administrator. Thus any general wage policy developed by the Board is subject to his approval. It is my understanding that Mr. Eric Johnston, while Economic Stabilization Administrator, leaned toward a general base-date kind of policy.

Since the meat packing decision we have also had to consider the General Motors type of annual productivity factor. That is another question which is on the fringe of a developing wage policy, and presents a challenge for the Board in the months ahead.

In conclusion, let me point out that we have two questions: whether or not we will have wage controls, and, if so, what kind of wage control program is desirable. On the first question, the National Association of Manufacturers and the United States Chamber of Commerce have taken the general position that indirect controls can do the job. I oppose that alternative because I think it inadequate to meet the menace of inflation. On the second question, I shall only express the hope that what I have said will indicate that, despite great difficulties, we have our heads pointed in the right direction.

A Case Study

Here is a case study drawn from the woolen and worsted business which may mean all the more because it puts into concrete, specific terms many of the implications of price and wage controls generally.

A number of occurrences have affected the prices in our industry. In June 1950 the government announced its intention of placing orders of large quantities of fabric for the various armed services. On October 1, 1950, a twelve-cent increase was granted to all worsted and woolen employees. In December 1950 Congress authorized the purchase of one hundred million pounds of wool for stockpiling purposes. (Domestic wool amounts to only about one-third of our total consumption in this country.) The announcement of stockpiling, along with the purchase by the government of fabric and wool, sent wool prices skyrocketing. For example, the price of a particular grade of wool for which we paid $2.00 per pound on June 1, 1950, reached $4.80 a pound on March 15, 1951.

Then on March 15, the government, at this point still one-third short of meeting the stockpile goal, decided to reduce its purchasing program. As a result, there was a severe recession in the wool market. The same grade of wool which had gone from $2.00 to $4.80 per pound dropped to $3.20. But the net increase over June 1950 was still large—in the nature of $1.20. Thus when we started with price control in our industry, we started on the basis of an unstabilized world commodity at an already high cost level—a level which rose substantially after price controls were imposed. Under such circumstances, the difficulties of working out ceiling prices which still permit a company to do business are quite apparent.

One of the major problems that is presented to our industry as a result of this commodity increase is how to finance a business when the values with which we must operate are so much greater than the historic values on which profitability is based. For example, our company, employing roughly five thousand people, normally does around forty million dollars of business. To maintain the same physical volume under the higher price of wool, we probably would have to do between sixty-five million and seventy million. But that is impossible, because we are not prepared to finance operations on such a scale. Therefore, we face the necessity of curtailing our production. And not only does this mean selling fewer items, with less chance to break even, but it is at variance with the idea, which I believe we all hold, that expansion of production is the final answer to the control of the price picture.

Moreover, our margins may be squeezed too. It is significant to note that for several months following March 1951, it was just impossible to sell a piece of goods in any of the textile trades of the country—cottons or rayons or wool products. As a result, of course, a wickedly low level of selling prices relative to cost prices has developed in our industry.

But there is another side to the problem that is equally serious. I was one of the men in industry who loudly claimed during the second World War that the end effect of OPA was to increase rather than decrease the price of some goods. The inability to write a flexible enough law to cover all cases cannot help but lead, in many instances, to the overpricing of merchandise. The same influence, in my opinion, is prevalent under OPS at the present time. Let me illustrate:

> The cost of manufacturing for woolens is much cheaper than that for worsteds; waste products and by-products of industry, as well as the shorter wools, can be used. So generally woolens are priced underneath worsteds goods and, as a result, serve as competition to worsteds.
>
> During the base period used by OPS, however, woolens were not in demand in this country, but worsteds were. The resulting terrific competition on woolens actually forced woolen prices below cost.
>
> So woolen mills, with ceiling prices set on a base period of nonprofit operation, are assured of a loss if they continue with exactly the same type of product today.
>
> The only "out" they have under the OPS formulas is to change over to products with a higher level of pricing and hence, generally, bigger dollar margins.

My conversations with many fellow businessmen confirm my observation that OPS is thus forcing higher prices in our industry. Of course, I cannot blame the OPS as such for making an over-all ruling; but I can find fault with it for failing to formulate details so that higher priced goods would not have such a premium over cheaper goods.

No wonder I feel that this country would be better off if business were free to set prices and wages according to competition rather than being controlled by the best laws that could be made. However, if we must have controls, then I feel that there are certain steps that OPS must take: (1) make a serious effort to work out a plan which will encourage the production of the lower priced lines of merchandise; (2) leave no stone unturned to encourage the highest possible production; (3) allow a fair margin of profit. These objectives are even more important from the standpoint of the public than from the standpoint of business. After all, most of our profits are recaptured in taxes, and the country needs tax money.

For the most part, I think we can rely on free competition to realize these objectives better than controls. Mr. Don Mitchell, President of Sylvania Products, recently remarked—somewhat facetiously but nonetheless to the point—that he had been acquainted during the second World War, and he was now, with the alphabetical names of the various agencies, but he rather thought that alphabetical names like GE and RCA did more to force his prices down than OPA and OPS.

As for the subject of wage controls, here, too, I feel that "hands off" is the best policy. It is too complicated to cover by over-all rules. One of the great problems in handling wages, of course, lies in the cost of labor in a finished item. In one item labor may amount to a fraction of 1 per cent of the total cost; in another it may run as high as 80 per cent. Obviously, then, a labor charge means much more to the manufacturers with the high percentage of labor in a finished article than to the manufacturer with the low labor cost in his article.

Again, to use my industry as an example, we have both large companies and small companies; we have the North and the South with their sectional differences; we also have differences, of course, between individual mills in a given community. How can all those differences be allowed for in a rule without hampering business?

After all, the success or the failure of our businesses depends upon ourselves, our research, our methods of handling people, our skill in purchasing, and so on. There lie the final answers as to whether this business lives or that business dies. And I am quite sure, as was indicated in the postwar period, that in only a very few cases would it be necessary to control labor and the wages of labor by government law.

Organized labor, as we all know, exerts a tremendous pressure upon government. Actually that is where the pressure is being applied, that is where the decision is going to be made, and American business cannot permit itself, if it is going to remain in free competition, to be regulated by government.

MATERIALS CONTROLS

Horace B. McCoy, Malcolm Slaght, Frank Lewis, Edward J. Hanley, and Eliot Janeway

INTRODUCTION

In going around the country recently I came to the conclusion that the largest amount of business worry seems to center in price controls. Apparently, they affect the pocketbook of business a little bit more, at present, than materials controls do.

Not only is it probably true that the part of the defense-mobilization program affecting materials has been less onerous (shall we say?) to business generally; it has also been almost completely unnoticed by the public in contrast to the other aspects of defense mobilization, notably wage stabilization, which have been the subject of conversation and discussion and acute interest. Yet there are signs pointing, as we will indicate in this chapter, to the fact that materials controls may become more significant, and their effect may begin to spread more noticeably, here and there, through the economy not too far in the future.

By this time we have had considerable experience in the control of defense materials for the defense program. The Defense Production Act was enacted in December 1950, and the government promptly went to work. Since this date a great deal has been done, a lot of ground has been covered and—representing the government, I can say this with due modesty, because we had the help of busi-

NOTE: Mr. McCoy is Assistant Administrator for Industry Operations, National Production Authority, Department of Commerce; Mr. Slaght is Director, Foreign Division of NPA; Mr. Lewis is Manager of Manufacturing, Home Appliance Division, General Electric Company; Mr. Hanley is President of the Allegheny Ludlum Steel Corp.; and Mr. Janeway is consultant, writer, and contributor to *Newsweek*.

The introduction and conclusion are drawn from Mr. McCoy's remarks; Mr. Slaght explains CMP from the government point of view; Mr. Lewis and Mr. Hanley represent two manufacturers' views; and Mr. Janeway makes the attempt to strike a balance.

ness—in a much shorter time, with much less dislocation, than was true of the last emergency.

Almost a year after the Korean outbreak—I am using figures as of the end of the first quarter of 1951—defense expenditures are about 8 per cent of our gross national product. As presently outlined and barring any substantial changes upward, our defense program at its height will take about one-fifth of our total economic effort, as measured by gross national product. (I believe the highest figure we ever reached during the second World War was 45 per cent.)

Our gross national product, in dollar terms, is the highest in history: 328 billion dollars per year at mid-1951, which is a 17 per cent increase over 1950. Though, of course, a large part of that increase has been due to rising prices, at least one-half of it represents physical volume of goods.

The labor force is at its highest peak. We now have about a million more people in the labor force and actually at work than we had last year. Unemployment is probably below the two million level. We have what to all intents and purposes in this country is full employment.

Against this background of high-level activity and the mandate of still further expansion of the economy for defense, we set up the first phase of controls, if you want to call them that. They were not, of course, controls in the full sense of the word. The so-called "D.O." system merely provided that defense (military) orders executed by the procurement agencies would get right of way over all other private contracts, and that the rest of the economy operated on what was left—no preferences, no allocations, no controls affecting business generally; all we had in mind was just a right of way for the military effort.

The second phase took place in early 1951. We supplemented the military ratings with preferences for certain elements in the economy that we considered "defense supporting" and which had to be lifted above the general level of all business.

Freight cars provide a good example. It was felt that our defense program required that we supply direct assistance to the production of freight cars, that we thus increase the production in that area above what it would normally be if left free.

Machine tools can serve as another example. Here is an industry which traditionally has ups and downs, and the inception of the defense program found the machine tool industry down in the cellar. It had to be brought up and brought up rapidly. We estimated that, while the annual output of machine tools around the middle of 1950 was perhaps 250 million dollars a year, to meet full military requirements foreseeable in 1951 and 1952 the industry would have to have an annual capacity, dollar-wise, of about 1.2 billion.

This was the second phase—moving into the nonmilitary area as distinguished from the strictly military, selecting certain crucial industries, and giving them special priorities (thus cutting down a little on the materials available for everyone else) so that those programs could be lifted to a higher level than the general economy.

The third phase is the one we have now entered. When we have gone a certain distance with defense-supporting priorities, we find that we must go just about all the rest of the way and allocate materials for all types of production. Just as soon as the point is reached where up to 50 per cent or 60 per cent or even 70 per cent of the total supply of materials is being allocated directly for specific purposes (military and defense-supporting), the free area diminishes in magnitude, and the pressures and the bargaining and scrambling for the balance of the materials become so great that we must cover that area, too—hence the Controlled Materials Plan (CMP).

So businessmen must expect a more-or-less complete control of the industrial economy through materials allocations and production directives. The use of production directives—in terms of specific products, quantities, times, and places—requires that some industries make certain changes in their production operations. For example, the steel industry was directed to change the mix of its product; some of the mills normally making cheap metal must make plate for freight cars.

Again, we had to set up controls to guide industrial expansion. Industry has proposed an expansion of capacity of such magnitude that we could not possibly supply the materials for all of it. So we license the types of facility to be constructed and give them materials in that order of priority, depending on their importance to our emergency situation.

Most of our present problems are of that nature. In other words, how do we divide the resources of the country among (1) direct military, (2) defense-supporting, and (3) purely civilian uses? Also, how do we relate the needs of those three major groups, not only one to the other but also within each of the three groups, including the third which involves purely civilian production? Is it necessary to determine how many automobiles are to be made against how many appliances and other items are to be made in that restricted area?

There are also problems of materials supply on the international level. The international conferences on materials which have been mentioned in the press have an important bearing on our future supply, which will depend—in some cases 100 per cent—on materials from abroad. That is especially true of some of the alloy materials.

And finally, but not least important, we have the problem of maintaining the position of small business and—to put it more broadly—of maintaining a strong economy. If we do not succeed in doing that, all our other efforts will fail.

CMP—Government Viewpoint

It would take one hundred pages to describe CMP in detail. So I propose in the space available to look only at the basic "how," "what," and "why" of the plan.

Perhaps it may be useful, if anyone has missed the forest for the trees, or perhaps the trees for the paper, to start out by noting that the history of CMP goes back in actual fact to 1941. Even before Pearl Harbor, in the summer of 1941, some of the government economists began to discuss allocations as a better means of control than a system of multiple priorities. Thus CMP had a very long period of gestation. There were many intermediate systems of control before it came into full operation many, many months later.

The concept of a multiple-band preference rating system is a very attractive one. In a period of national stress, when national objectives are well-known, we simply arrange, on a scale from one to a hundred, the urgencies of everything the country makes. We graduate a beaker, if you like, and put the atom bomb on the bottom, jet planes next, and mark it off all the way up, with nonessentials like Christmas tree decorations at the top. We pour all our materials and facilities into this beaker. Of course, there is not enough to fill it. Presumably, our materials and facilities are completely utilized, and we have supplied the most urgent jobs. At least that was the concept in the very early days of our efforts to develop a control system.

Now that theory, as it was very early discovered, breaks down for two reasons:

(1) Any radical change in the product mix within the economy—and such a change is always involved in any period of stress of the kind we are speaking of—creates acute shortages of one material or component and no shortages of another. Consequently, the picture of materials filling the beaker evenly up to a certain level does not hold true. Instead, we get half-finished products of all kinds the whole way up the scale—the classic case of trucks without wheels.

(2) Even more seriously, the theory of priorities itself is fallacious. In a period of emergency, there is no such thing as an absolute urgency of one item of production over another item. Consider rifles and streetcars. The need for a given production of rifles cannot take precedence over the need for repair parts for streetcars if the latter are required to take the workers to the plants to build the rifles. So we must cut back the rifle program to get the steel for the streetcars. The actual objective is to achieve the kind of balance in the entire output of the economy which will contribute most to national objectives, which, in time of war, are very clear and even now, though less clear-cut, can still be objectively stated.

In other words, judgments must be quantitative. That is why a priorities system, which is qualitative, breaks down. CMP, on the other hand, does provide a mechanism for quantitatively determining what will be produced by our economy. It does more than that; it also provides a mechanism for ensuring that end units will come off the production line whole—not airplane wings with nothing to put in between, not trucks without wheels, not all the other incomplete products which plagued us in 1941 and early 1942.

The method that CMP uses is the allocation of copper, steel, and aluminum. CMP's function is to control, to schedule production; the allocation of copper, steel, and aluminum is only the mechanism through which it operates. Many alternatives to copper, steel, and aluminum—other production yardsticks—were considered both during the second World War and again this time, as for example dollars, labor hours, and kilowatt hours. All these alternatives offer certain advantages under some conditions, but the three basic metals seem to provide the flat control of production under conditions of high output of military weapons. They proved effective during the late years of the last war; after a very serious review, we decided that we could do no better this time.

CMP accomplishes its job of scheduling by dividing the industrial world into "A" and "B" products. As a matter of fact, the length of time it took to bring out CMP during the last war was largely a matter of developing this concept of "A" and "B" products. We had, for a long time, a group who wanted to handle everything as "A" products. We had another group who wanted to handle everything as "B" products; in fact, we used such a system for quite a while. But neither an "A" nor a "B" system will work by itself, and the real brilliance of the inventors of CMP was to reconcile these two schools of thought by combining them.

An "A" product is anything which is manufactured to specification—ordinarily from a blueprint—with some exceptions, of course. A "B" product is any item which is manufactured for stock—again with some exceptions. In the case of "A" products, the end-item manufacturer gets an authorized production schedule plus a complete allotment of materials (with preference ratings), out of which he in turn covers his subcontractors and subsubcontractors to the extent they are making components to his special order. In the case of "B" products or "shelf items," the producers, who must of necessity manufacture ahead of specific demands, get their authorized production schedules and allotments of materials directly from NPA on the basis of the total demand of the economy for their products, computed from indirect evidence rather than on the basis of specific contracts.

Our objective, at the present time, is certainly not to bleed the civilian economy in order to produce weapons to lick an enemy. The size of our total contemplated military program, as Mr. McCoy points out, does not approach the percentage of total national product that it reached in the second World War. At the same time, the problem of maintaining the civilian economy this time is greater because of the smaller number of men in the armed services, the indefinite duration of our problems, and other reasons. Yet CMP is adaptable to this problem; its mechanism is flexible, and it can be used to control the American industrial economy so long as there are national objectives which require that it be controlled.

We have now moved into CMP, and we shall continue to use it more and more. The only basic difference from the CMP of the last war is the way we are starting. As a matter of fact, at no point during the last eight months have there been any real questions in Washington about the ultimate need for CMP. The arguments, rather, have centered around these points: How do we get to CMP? When do we start? How do we handle the transition quarter?

The difficulties, when one first looks at the details of these problems, are almost past belief. But the worst will soon be over. We in Washington hope that the business community will be just a little lenient in its judgment until things settle down.

Two Manufacturers' Views

I should like simply to make a few comments and to raise a few questions with respect to CMP which will, I hope, lead to better understanding of this most important subject from the manufacturer's point of view.

CMP presents the best way to assure an equitable distribution of steel, copper, and aluminum to essential civil and defense production. A few words of caution are in order, however, when considering the plan as a whole and its relation to regular methods of operating in a free and open materials market. CMP is offered to manufacturers as an aid to their operations, and it must never be considered a panacea to the ills and troubles that are inevitable under operating conditions as we find them today. Therefore, in my opinion there are no substitutes for good production planning, aggressive and economical purchasing, careful scheduling for uniform output, and a continuous program toward the conservation of critical materials, combined with substitution of less critical materials wherever possible.

I represent the small apparatus manufacturing divisions of the General Electric Company. In these divisions we manufacture a varied line of products:

Integral and fractional HP motors
Industrial controls
Specialty transformers and ballasts
Meters and instruments
Industrial ovens and heating devices
Street lights
Flood lights
Rectifiers
Welding equipment

Fortunately, almost without exception these products are included in the unasterisked list of "B" products contained in the official CMP tabulation. Hence, all these products are used by and are essential to defense and civil programs presently planned to meet the requirements of an economy directed toward both peace and war.

You have probably said to yourselves, "How good or how bad is this plan for my business? What are the advantages and disadvantages of such a plan?"

As for advantages, I think we can all agree that CMP will assure essential manufacturing organizations an adequate supply of steel, copper, and aluminum to meet plant production schedules which are reasonably consistent with the output rates of late 1950 and early 1951 operations.

CMP permits a manufacturer to extend D.O. ratings to all of his suppliers of these materials and to suppliers of others, including components and subassemblies.

It recognizes the importance of a proper balance between defense and civil needs to the end that a high level of employment and industrial output is maintained.

Now, realizing that few, if any, plans can achieve perfection, I believe we should point out and discuss some of the obvious disadvantages on an objective basis with the hope that discussion will develop ideas and improvements toward a better operation of CMP. This is most important in the event that it becomes necessary to operate under this plan for an extended period of time.

My greatest concern, which is shared by our staff and the several operating managers at our factories, can be best presented by the questions we are receiving daily:

How closely is this plan geared to the critical materials limitation orders?

Can we obtain sufficient quantities of other critical materials, such as cobalt, nickel, tin, lead, zinc, chemicals for plastics, and so on, even though CMP ratings can be extended?

Why is the plan open-ended?

Is it practical or possible to control a portion of the metal market and leave the balance to operate without restrictions?

In the event of a swing toward war or a larger defense program, has consideration been given to an end use or priority system in connection with CMP so that essentiality or requirement patterns can be more clearly established?

My comments are related to a particular business within the electrical industry. But the same general questions might be asked by all industries.

• • •

Those of us in the steel business, the high alloy steel business at least, have been greatly concerned with material shortages since September 1950, when pressure on the International Nickel Company became so great that it had to allocate its nickel products on the basis of past requirements. Cobalt and columbium joined the critical list very quickly, and thereafter other materials have followed.

Users of high nickel steels or chrome-nickel steels have been kept supplied since September 1950 very largely through the ingenuity and ability of those in the metallurgical and production departments of the mills. Nickel has been resurrected from all kinds of sources. At our plants, for instance, the amount of nickel that has been recovered from scrap and grinder dust is a great tribute to the ingenuity of the metallurgists. As a matter of fact, from 40 per cent to 50 per cent of the nickel that we consumed in the first quarter of 1951 came from such sources, rather than from our supplier of primary nickel. Furthermore, by controlling very strictly the analyses of our steels and thereby keeping the quantities of critical alloys used to the barest minimum, we have stretched our supplies considerably.

In the meantime, it has been possible to make further substitutions for the conventional chrome-nickel stainless steels. For example, straight chrome steel is used today in place of chrome-nickel steel to an extent which a year ago would have been thought impossible. When the emergency is over, some of these users will swing back to chrome-nickel steels; but, on the other hand, I suspect that more straight chrome will be used as a result of the experience now being gained.

One question bothers me very much. Critical alloys seem to be in shorter supply now than during the second World War, and one wonders whether the end uses for these critical materials are being adequately examined and screened.

When demand far exceeds supply, and prices are prevented from moving up to affect demand, it becomes necessary, of course, to direct the flow of materials. This is unfortunate because equitably directing the flow of materials is a practical impossibility. It was difficult during the second World War when we were interested primarily in prosecuting the war; it will be many times worse in the so-called "guns and butter" economy. I suppose we must have something like CMP. The Controlled Materials Plan worked quite well during the second World War, but it only worked because requirements were carefully determined and supply was then geared to those requirements through its use.

Another question concerns me also. Will we ever be rid of CMP now that we are in it? It was a war-time measure the last time, and when the war was over, controls were terminated. Now, however, we are adopting controls even though we are not involved in a large-scale war. The war program is really quite small in respect to its requirements for military needs. During the first quarter of 1951, for example, only 8 per cent of the demand was required for the military. Yet, strangely enough, we seem to have just about run out of everything already.

Incidentally, much of the present requirement for steel is for plants to be used a year or two hence to make apparatus for war. In order to see if sufficient alloys are available for the ultimate production job therefore, we must look not only at the present situation but also at what it will be when these plants are operating. If we are out of materials now, where will we be then?

It is obvious that I am doubtful as to the thoroughness with which current and future requirements for material have been examined. A thorough analysis would seem to be necessary (1) to determine if CMP is really essential at this time, and (2) to provide the fundamental groundwork which will permit CMP to function properly if it is necessary.

On Balance

The distinction between today's emergent crisis and the situation presented us by Pearl Harbor is more than academic. The initiative of others having set the limits and objectives of war before we had to begin fighting it, we had no alternative but to mobilize as fully and as fast as possible. In that situation, it was necessary to arm by throttling the civilian economy down drastically. Given a longer war, this might have proved even more dangerous than a slower rate of war production. As it happened, the errors of our enemies and the initiative, the resources, and the sacrifices of our allies implemented our own achievements in time to give us the quick victory required by our forced commitment to maximal war production and to minimal civilian production.

How thoroughly our lack of political initiative, before the last war, ended by depriving us of the initiative in production planning is illustrated by the fact that we never did program civilian production.

Before Pearl Harbor the civilian officials in charge of protecting civilian needs were the ones who took the responsibility in pressing for an accelerated rate of conversion of durable goods facilities to war production. For the duration the civilian economy was regarded as a bottomless grab bag from which to pick the ingredients of war production when and as needed. At no time were civilian requirements budgeted on either a rock-bottom basis—to prevent a decline in war production—or on the expanding scale required to support a longer and bigger war than we actually won.

As it happened, the civilian economy was more than adequate to support the load thrust upon it. This does not mean that it can support the immeasurably greater load that is likely to be thrust upon it this time. Nor does it mean that we should again mobilize as if the requirements of war production could be calculated with no concern for the supporting or reciprocally expanding requirements of the civilian economy. On pain of undermobilizing for the long struggle ahead, we must be wary of rushing into crippling commitments to over-mobilize for immediate psychological relief.

Mobilization today presupposes an intense and professional study of the experience of the second World War for the twin purpose of clarifying what wants to be repeated and what wants to be avoided. Inescapably, every decision discussed today is being considered in the light of policies and experiments adopted last time. In the main, this reflects a healthy effort to profit from experience by applying it to new problems. But it also exposes us to the temptation of operating blindly and narrowly by the "experiential fallacy," which can be quite as mischievous as the opposite error of ignoring experience. In no area is it more important to study the experience of the last war in order to avoid following it than in that staked out by the civilian economy.

Fortunately, one of the most penetrating students of our home-front experience in the second World War happens to have played a strategic role in setting the pattern of production planning in 1950–1951. Manly Fleischmann has already proved himself to be a wise and effective production administrator. But if he had not taken hold as Administrator of the National Production Authority, he would still have made a place for himself as an expert on the subject by the definitive contribution he published late in the second World War in collaboration with John Lord O'Brian, his chief as General Counsel of the War Production Board. "The War Production Board Administrative Policies and Procedures" (*George Washington Law Review,* December 1944) is at once a comprehensive review of recurring fundamentals and a searching evaluation of experience and expedients to be remembered, not least in respect of the need for intergearing between military and civilian requirements.

Fleischmann's own summary of his past and present experience on this score should be taken as a model of practical wisdom. "If I had to choose between an allocation for the hundred-thousandth tank in a Detroit arsenal," he says, "and the same allocation to maintain the New York water supply, I would divert the allocation from the arsenal to the water works." This should be taken as axiomatic come the terrible day when such administrative dilemmas may be upon us. The equally compelling corollary is that we must pursue a course now which will minimize the pressure upon us to make such crippling choices.

Such pressure is being felt already. The critical list of strategic materials in short supply is a long and ominous one. It begins with rubber, tin, tungsten, nickel, platinum, copper, lead, manganese, chrome, wool, vegetable oils, chemicals; inevitably and monotonously, the shortages have appeared where they will always appear unless and until stockpiling and preventive expansion combine to anticipate them.

Here, experience has sufficed no more than on the eve of Pearl Harbor. One of the most urgent problems confronting mobilization today is that of expediting and of expanding the flow of strategic imports and absorbing it into the broader flow of production. On the one hand, Price Director Michael DiSalle recognizes, and has told the State Department, that the domestic price structure cannot be stabilized in the absence of effective international price stabilization. On the other hand, importers, harassed between shortages of these critical items and domestic price controls, are understandably reluctant to contract for the shipments the country needs. Altogether, shortages of strategic imports are imposing an unanticipated and intolerable ceiling on American production while, at the same time, they are frustrating all efforts to impose ceilings on American production costs.

This is precisely the kind of pinch on the economy which we have not learned to anticipate and from which we must now free ourselves if we are to cope with the "crisis-process" during the years to come. Only a multiplicity of world-wide expansion projects, undertaken as part of a parallel program to negotiate intergovernmental stabilization of the cost of strategic goods and services, will enable us to do so. But such off-shore expansion projects, elaborate and expensive as they must be, will have the effect, at least over the short term, of sharpening the present pinch on both military programs and civilian supplies. For, if these shortages have been strait-jacketing production below the level of requirements, the job of breaking foreign production and financial bottlenecks and insuring an increasing flow of imports will load an additional burden upon domestic capacities set aside for essential programs. We shall have to pay for these imports with exports of equipment and goods already under allocation; and, in every case, we shall have to make the investment in exports long before we can expect to receive the return.

The import pinch and the inescapable export burden on requirements needed to ease it between them cut across the delicate area connecting the war and civilian sectors of the economy. The changed status of lead illustrates how the import pinch is increasing the dependence of each sector upon the other:

During the second World War we managed without automobile production and with gasoline rationing. Also, we were not under serious pressure to divert capacities into civilian-defense installations. Accordingly, radical curtailment of civilian demand for gasoline and automobile storage batteries reduced lead requirements, while our freedom from attack avoided any need for its use in shelters.

Today, by contrast, our vulnerability to atomic attack gives us every incentive to keep the country on wheels if only because we cannot indefinitely avoid shifting installations to areas relatively remote from target centers; and, as noted, gasoline and automobiles require lead. We also need tremendous new supplies of lead for shelters in target areas. In addition, lead—for insulation—has emerged as a prime requirement in atomic programs.

Finally, the lead load is being increased by the pressure to reduce the still more critical tin load, which means that effective measures of tin conservation must provide for no less effective measures of lead expansion.

Thus, to protect the integrity of our military and atomic programs, we must guarantee significant increases in lead supplies to the civilian economy; and this we can only do by depriving present military programs of materials and machinery needed to expand lead production here and abroad.

In this respect, we will do well to copy the procedure adopted by the War Production Board during the last war. Its Controlled Materials Plan—*to be differentiated sharply from the loose term used nowadays to describe more or less planned ways of imposing more or less control on any and all materials (including the so-called "open-end" CMP established July 1, 1951)*—gave Allied military allocations full and equal priority with American military allocations, and also guaranteed civilian exports as much protection as any domestic civilian claimants upon the economy enjoyed. We have yet to adopt this procedure.

The reason why we have not is inherent in the evolution of our remobilization. We are still in the stage corresponding to the long and costly siege in the second World War before the collapse of the priority system forced the adoption of the Controlled Materials Plan. The priority system, as introduced before Pearl Harbor and operative until the end of 1942, builds requirements up piecemeal by the process of recognizing individual pressures. Its weakness is that it exposes administrators to the temptation to issue priorities as fast as claimants press for them, while it gives the manufacturers of everything from electric locomotives to slot machines a practical competitive incentive for seeking priority status as more or less essential to more or less essential functions.

By contrast, the Controlled Materials Plan, as formulated and pioneered by Ferdinand Eberstadt, proceeds from the general to the particular, from the budgeting of over-all requirements to the scheduling of indicated end-uses. We have it on the authority of Eberstadt—who, let it be remembered, was maligned as a "militarist" prejudiced against the civilian function in a war economy—that civilian requirements, with special emphasis on civilian foreign trade and foreign trade expanding requirements, should be budgeted for as prime war-economy claimants. To do so, however, assumes that military requirements can be calculated and have been calculated.

The priority system, which has been the only alternative open to us up to this point, grants claims upon the economy in response to pressure. While it remains operative, it is probable that civilian exports will continue to be by-passed in favor of domestic claimants scrambling for at least all the supplies in prospect. Not until this round robin of pressure has collapsed into priorities inflation, as it did after Pearl Harbor, can the budgeting process (always granting that military budgeters know for what to budget) ration disappointed claimants down to a level at which allowance can be made for foreign trade to be protected and for the import flow to expand.

Our economy, meanwhile, instead of expanding in the wake of increasing imports, is suffering severe dislocation and is being threatened with actual contraction in sensitive sectors for lack of imports in sufficient volume. And while the ceiling which strategic shortages have imposed upon our productive capacities is pressing down upon our economy, the demands of the military are squeezing it at the other end. Military requirements by definition always tend to be inflated. This is by no means as bad as it sounds, if only because inflation of military requirements invariably spurs necessary expansion of steel, aluminum, and other basic productive facilities.

In any case, there are many reasons why, in such a situation as the present, military requirements should be inflated. First and foremost is the overriding pressure of uncertainty. The halfway house between peace and war which we inhabit inevitably makes for exaggeration and duplication of requirements. The circumstances of our mobilizing for what Roosevelt would have called a very "iffy" war are understandably resulting in a process of bargaining between the civilians and the military over no less "iffy" requirements.

If over-all military requirements are "iffy," hence by definition inflated, those military requirements involving basic critical materials are unfortunately all too definite; in fact, the claims embodied in the sixty billion dollar military budget of mid-1951 assumed an availability for American military purposes alone of nickel, tungsten, and the like hopelessly in excess of prospective supplies available to the entire world. The pressure of arithmetic has dictated drastic deflation of these military requirements down into line with our ability to support armament while stimulating the expansion of chemical, metallurgical, and other "defense supporting" industries without gutting the civilian economy.

Clearly, the alloying materials on the critical list are to be viewed as constituting the lowest common denominator setting the effective limit past which production may not rise regardless of the availability of plant capacity, of manpower, and of supplies in relative surplus. The Russians appear to have taken over from the Germans metallurgical formulae for producing jet engines with little or no dependence on nickel. That we have not is well known. Until we do, our ability to produce jet engines will depend less upon the familiar press releases as to our commanding steel-ingot capacity than upon our success in obtaining nickel to alloy with the particular ingots of steel set aside for jet schedules.

A vicious circle, therefore, has been set in motion and must be broken. Because the military are working from no strategic plan susceptible of quantitative reduction to requirements, requirements are inflated at a time when the economy is dislocated by shortages. But because the economy is dislocated by shortages, any level of military requirements too high to permit the economy to expand is an inflated level.

How radically military requirements must expand in order to convert America into a relatively defensible theater of war is indicated by the fact that virtually all new military and atomic installations are being concentrated in "target" areas in order to keep supporting civilian requirements at a minimum, while no serious start has been made in relocating installations for the purpose of diversifying existing targets; and even the Atomic Energy Commission is obliged to locate its developments within economically transmittable reach of existing power facilities, i.e., in target areas. Clearly, any serious reorientation of requirements to prepare America's productive machinery for war is bound to multiply the mobilization load upon the civilian sector of the war economy.

Meanwhile, however, because military requirements (inflated or not) are "iffy," we are muddling along with a priority system. To be sure, it has begun to evolve toward the Controlled Materials Plan technique and now has even been given the same name. But here's the rub: before our admittedly transitional priority system can evolve into a real revived Controlled Materials Plan, military requirements must be reduced to measurable production schedules which are supportable by a civilian economy obliged to expand basic resources—extractive, utility, manufacturing, distributive—at home and abroad. The Controlled Materials Plan is the indispensable tool we need to deflate military requirements at the rate needed to program the expansion of basic resources. Unfortunately, however, a priority system, such as that we are improvising, is a most inefficient tool for this purpose. Says Manly Fleischmann of the second World War's pre-CMP priority system:

> [Its] principal defect . . . and one which eventually hastened its demise, was that it provided no mechanism for compelling the Army and Navy and other procuring agencies to reduce their production programs in accordance with the allotments given their prime and subcontractors.

Manly Fleischmann, therefore, is certainly being afforded a rare opportunity to apply a formative experience of the last war to today's crisis. He saw and studied closely the processes by which a hopelessly inflated priority system was converted into an efficient Controlled Materials Plan—under conditions clarified by a simple and definite strategic plan. As he noted in his article, a major obstacle in the way of this transition was the difficulty experienced by the civilian administrators of the inflated priority system in deflating military requirements down to controllable proportions.

Today, the priority system he is administering with such eloquently prophetic and prayerful misgivings is not yet hopelessly inflated, but inflation is in prospect for it. Professionally skillful and persistent bargaining has squeezed a great deal of water out of the military budget, but not enough. The question is whether a supportable schedule of requirements can be settled upon before priority inflation aggravates present dislocations and while we have the time and the mobility to substitute civilian expansion of basic resources for requirements inflation.

Fundamentally, the basic military requirement is the maximum reservoir of civilian resources. Certainly, any deflation of military requirements which supports an expansion of the over-all reservoir sets in motion a cycle of expanding military requirements. The most obvious illustration is a deflation of the primary military requirement —manpower—which grants small and temporary draft exemptions for the purpose of installing productive facilities able to support larger permanent draft schedules without risking curtailment of production.

We need all the expansion we can get right now to break the bottlenecks in the way of armament production. To control the flow of production today, it is not enough to regulate steel, aluminum, and copper, as CMP did in the second World War. We must apply the CMP technique to the critical materials which have come to constitute the lowest common denominator of American security. The present ceiling limiting American production will be raised as fast as we succeed in expanding the supply of the bottleneck items on the critical list.

Conclusion

Some businessmen may question whether the military will actually cut their requirements (that is, authorized production schedules under CMP) down to the level required by the shortage of critical alloys. Otherwise, of course, CMP would not work.

I recall that in the first full month in which the D.O. system was operating, the D.O.'s, which were at least alleged to be for direct military production, added up to the total supply available for that month. We simply cut those in half and allocated only 50 per cent.

We never heard anything from it, so we assumed that businessmen were ordering considerably in advance—not hoarding, of course, but merely "protecting" themselves.

Actually, CMP is supposed to take water out of lead times, to pin industry down to the inventory needed for authorized production programs, and to make those two match precisely and on time. It is much more effective in the control of inventory than our regular inventory order, which says, in effect, "Use your own conscience about your inventory, although you can be prosecuted under Regulation 1 for having more inventory."

Will the military cut down their schedules? They will have to, because their allotment in these very short alloys will be made on an over-all basis to meet not only military and defense-supporting but also essential civilian production. We would have no electronic industry at all today if we did not take nickel out of the general supply and put it into the electronic industry. There would be no incandescent light industry operating unless we drew tungsten out of the general supply; and the military demands have to be adjusted to it.

So, I repeat, we are cutting back and will continue to cut back the military demands wherever necessary.

Another point which concerns businessmen—and a good one with which to close—is the question of when we can abandon CMP.

In the case of some materials, notably steel and aluminum, we have active programs to expand production. Our probable over-all steel expansion represents an increase from, roughly, one hundred million ingot tons in January 1950 to perhaps one hundred and twenty million tons by the end of 1952. Aluminum has been expanded likewise. It is very likely that we shall reach our military objectives in 1952 and, if not then, certainly in early 1953. At that point there should be an adequate supply to meet all needs, and hence no reason for allocations by the government.

Take rubber as an example. We have a large stockpile objective for natural rubber. By the time that is achieved—I do not know just when, but let us assume in late 1952—there will be a total of maybe 900,000 tons of synthetic rubber available, plus imports of at least 700,000 tons of natural rubber; that adds up to a quantity of new rubber in excess of any consumption rate we have ever had in this country. Obviously, there is no need of controls under those conditions.

I do not pretend to know enough to predict the course of controls. In 1946 we began to take off controls in rather a big hurry. Few remained in 1947 and 1948. Rubber continued under control, but for a different purpose—to maintain by law a source of rubber in this country, i.e., the facility to produce synthetic rubber. Whether the same situation will apply this time is hard to tell. However, I look forward, personally, to the fact that we may be able to remove controls from some materials in late 1952, and certainly from most of the more important ones by 1953, but that is a very hazardous type of guess at the moment.

ORGANIZING PRODUCTION PERSONNEL

Franklin E. Folts, Roger Lowell Putnam, and John D. Glover

Lessons from the Second World War

In thinking ahead about the problems posed by the defense effort —whether for an emergency situation like that of Korea, or a period of uneasy preparation between crises, or the imminence of all-out war—one of the best guides is our experience in the second World War. Let me point out a few of the things I think we can—and must —learn from that experience in the vital area of organizing production personnel.

Our ability to develop and maintain a dual military-civilian program depends upon industry's capacity to produce. This, in turn, is determined not only by the supply of facilities (plant, machines, and so forth) and the supply of materials, but also by the supply of qualified supervisory people and workers.

The experience of the last war demonstrates that the supply of supervisors and workers can constitute a bottleneck, can put a definite ceiling on the output of an individual company or operation. In the years immediately ahead of us will not workers and supervisors again represent one of the most difficult supply spots?

We are all of us perfectly aware, I am sure, that the problems of obtaining and developing and holding an adequate supervisory organization and work force are with us right now; there is no question about that. We also should be aware of the fact that those problems inevitably are going to be more acute as time goes on, and that finally in the event of all-out war our ability to solve the problems of

NOTE: Mr. Folts is Professor of Industrial Management, Harvard Business School; Mr. Putnam is President, Package Machinery Company, Springfield, Massachusetts; and Mr. Glover is Associate Professor of Business Administration, Harvard Business School.

Mr. Folts sets forth the lessons of the second World War; Mr. Putnam and Mr. Glover explore the problems of morale and communication, respectively.

the supervisory organization and work force is likely to be the measure of our industrial effort and contribution to victory.

At the same time, we are in a relatively better position to cope with these problems than in the last war—for four reasons:

1. The last war showed us much in the way of what to do and how to do it.

2. The last war gave us quite a kit of management tools to work with in dealing with such problems.

3. Experience *since* the last war has enlarged that kit substantially and given us still more tools to work with.

4. Also our postwar experience has shown us much about what we did *in error* last time. If we will listen to that experience, perhaps we may avoid some of the problems this time.

Let me start with the question of what the last war actually showed us that can be useful to us now.

(1) The first and perhaps the most important lesson of all is that our second World War experience certainly ought to convince every one of us that taking things as they come and acting by expediency only wastes time in the end. We must anticipate our problems. Now is the time to act, not a month from now or three months from now or six months from now. There is no doubt about it: we are fortunate to have an opportunity to get ready this time. So why not take advantage of it?

(2) Another lesson that the war taught us is that we can increase the productivity of a work force through the reorganization of the work itself and through careful selection of people to do this kind of job and that kind of job—trying to keep the skilled people exclusively on skilled jobs and utilizing the unskilled workers that come into the work force on other jobs for which they can be trained more readily. In so doing, we count on the fact that an emergency situation justifies the organization of work in ways that would hardly be tolerated in a nonemergency situation. (That is one of the reasons why the potential output in our work force is greater under an emergency situation than it is under normal conditions.)

We can take that lesson and follow it closely. It was good then.

It will work now—provided, of course, we go ahead and add to what we learned the last time.

To achieve this fuller utilization of the work force we must train and train and train. The increased role of training, as I have observed it, is the best thing that happened to industry as the result of the last war. Training really applies in the present situation. (It probably applies for all time, as far as that is concerned.) So now is the time to replan jobs, both worker jobs and supervisory jobs—and not only to plan, but as a matter of fact, even before the situation becomes acute, to undertake a great deal of the actual training.

(3) A third lesson that the last war taught us is that the effect of what we do in an emergency stays with us a long time after the victory is won and the emergency is over. Apparently we did not understand that the last time, but we certainly have an opportunity to understand it now. I know of quite a number of places where today we are still paying the price for the things we did wrong.

Let me give a few simple, very earthy illustrations of what we did wrong the last time and must avoid this time. Take the following well-known sequence:

(a) As soon as abnormal demand for labor is felt, wages go up.
(b) Then we get a wage freeze as an anti-inflationary measure.
(c) That puts a stop to the use of relatively high wages as a means of attracting labor to our plants.

But does the wage freeze do what it is supposed to do—put a stop to the rapid upward spiral of wages, the pirating of labor from one shop to another shop through attractively higher and higher wages, and so on? Unfortunately, the last time a good many people found ways and means of circumventing this wage-fixing situation very neatly and very nicely:

1. *If the job was on piece rate,* we changed the job in such a way as to liberalize the time standards; that is, we fixed the job so that the worker could perform it in less time than the standard called for.

We did this by giving him more tools or better tools; or we did it by cutting down on the job, omitting such things as inspection by the worker, machine maintenance, or the repair of the worker's defective work.

Or we went in the opposite direction—including work that was not in the job before and at the same time increasing the time allowance for the performance of the job out of proportion to the new duties added. The effect of such action was of course that the worker got more money for doing less work.

A simpler approach to this problem was to condone the padding of worker output reports used for payroll purposes.

In fact, management does not need to *do* any of these things. Just leave the situation alone, and the first thing you know the workers and supervisors will have done them of their own accord. Management can of course speed up the process by making suggestions.

2. *If it was an hourly paid job,* we found that we could add to the job in simple ways and at the same time could put it into a higher pay classification. Asking the worker to inspect every tenth piece produced, for example, was an effective way of doing this. The fact that the job was immediately thereafter subject to a 100 per cent inspection by the inspection department did not matter. And if the worker realized that this inspection was going to take place very soon and so neglected to perform his additional assignment, perhaps that did not matter either—if the purpose was to get around the wage freeze.

Another approach was to simplify the job by breaking it into parts so that less skilled labor would be used, at the same time keeping the job in its old pay classification. Here, again, workers and foremen will take the initiative if they are simply left alone.

In other words, a wage freeze does not necessarily stop the use of monetary compensation as a means of attracting workers and holding them, but if management takes advantage of that fact as just outlined, it must face the consequences.

There are always influences that can be depended upon to "liberalize" worker compensation under wartime conditions—particularly the softening of standards and slackening of control devices. In the main these influences are with us always, but normal competition tends to hold them in check, whereas the wartime economy, emphasizing output and de-emphasizing price, tends to release them.

The consequences show up in the struggles that many companies have gone through since the war in trying to get worker productivity back up to what they think of as a normal level, judged by what it was before the war. One can find plenty of soft time standards that were set up during the war, just as one can find too liberal job classifications, and, believe me, it is not easy to tighten them up.

This is not a matter of honesty or dishonesty. If management condones a dishonest practice on the part of workers by paying the inflated wages, it does not take long before that practice no longer is dishonest. As far as the workers are concerned, it is now a rule of the game; that is all.

Obviously, what is needed more than ever is an adequate standards department. In peacetime there is no problem; we naturally emphasize this activity because of its cost-reduction function. But when war industry expands payrolls and the number and kinds of jobs, we do not do what we should, which is to increase standards (time-study) departments proportionately. In fact, we commonly reduce them, because we need people very badly for line supervision.

There is no sense in pulling standards men and control people out of their functional jobs to put them into line jobs simply because of the need for line supervision. I know there is need of line supervision; I know too that the need will be much greater before we get through. But it is a fundamental mistake to try to get that line supervision by bleeding the control organization or the standards organization of its best men. Line foremen are important; that is right. But in the long run standards people and control people are, if anything, more important. It takes time to train competent standards and control men; there are no short cuts.

The result—unless positive action is taken to avoid it—is that the standards department becomes quite inadequate.

But it is not enough for the standards department itself to be adequate in size and ability; it is also imperative that top management support the standards department. If top management does not do that, the right job just is not going to be done, and the eventual result will be soft standards—no matter how good the standards are to start with.

While in peacetime management is quite consistently cost-minded and usually gives the standards department full backing on this account, in wartime there is always a temptation to liberalize "just a little." And when management says to itself, "Well, maybe we can afford to be just a little bit liberal," we can be sure that the standards are going to start down hill. The first to recognize this "just a little liberality" are the workers and the men in the standards department. Like "just a little pregnancy," it does not take long for it to have its effect. It shows fast.

Management pressures for quick results coupled with department shorthandedness mean that the time-study and methods men simply do not have time to do the job expected of them. What do they do under those conditions? Reach into the bag. The advice of the experienced time-study man who has gone through a wartime situation is consistently: "Be liberal. Being liberal is more friendly; it is easier; it is quicker." Poorly trained and/or inexperienced standards men quickly learn to err on the liberal side, too.

Thus, if top management does not stiffen the spine of its standards department and then back it up to the fullest degree, it may be sure that its standards will become progressively softer.

It is important that the foremen also support the standards department. Normally in peacetime we all know the foreman is under constant pressure to keep his costs in line, and he therefore tends to be on the standard man's side in any controversy over standards. But the moment he finds himself in the position where he is fighting for output, he is likely to do an about-face. "Keep the men happy and keep the work rolling out" becomes the new theme.

That is something to watch for. The only way that I know of to prevent it is by careful training of the supervisory force to instill in them the right spirit and right attitude toward job standards and toward wage-payment methods. Here, again, action should be taken immediately.

I could go on and on with illustrations of slipshod practices. All too often they were resorted to or slipped into during the last war;

and as the demand for labor increases with the growth of our foreseeable preparedness effort, they are very likely to be with us again.

Now, I have no intention of raising questions of ethics, of the impact of such practices on the economy, or of their social significance—all important as these matters are. I want to stay right down on the lowly level of operating supervisors and operating management and point out that when the conditions which bring about these maladjustments in wages and wage structure eventually disappear, their results—unjustifiable wage relationships and levels—do not disappear. *They stay right on with us.*

Today we are still paying the price for our wage malpractices of the last war. War-inflated job standards still are prevalent. Rate differentials in relation to job content in many, many cases are unrealistic. Too many standards men still remember the attitude of management and supervision back in those overworked days and take what they call a "realistic" attitude toward their function, which oftentimes is less "scientific" today than it was ten years ago, and it was bad enough then.

I have recently read a careful study of a dozen companies that have attempted complete revisions of their job standards and wage-rate structures since the war. The results range all the way down from success to complete failure; and, sadly enough, the successes seem to be in the minority.

Just because we are still paying the price today for our failure to face up to the unsoundness of some of the things we did the last time, however, is no reason to compound those errors if we do not have to. Now we know the importance of planning in a way we did not know the last time; now we know more about what needs to be planned and how to plan it than we knew the last time.

For all of us the experience of the second World War and the adjustment period that followed it is rich in advice for the immediate future. Job planning, standards setting, worker training, supervisor training, technician training, emergency policy determination and definition—all these are things that can and should be done now.

Fortunately we have many good management tools that we did not have at the start last time. Training Within Industry (TWI), with its subsidiary programs, is readily available to us. Other training aids are legion.

There are new developments in standards setting. Methods-Time-Measurement (MTM) is a technique for quickly setting realistic job standards without the use of a stop watch. Frequently it permits the setting of a standard before the job has even been performed. This is important.

Since the second World War considerable study has been made of what constitutes a fair day's work, and, despite the objections of some organized labor people, standards of a fair day's work are beginning to emerge. The recently released films on rating put out by the Society for Advancement of Management may well be a significant contribution in this area.

In other words, there is much that can be done to avoid some of the production-level problems of the last war effort. And also we know what some of the aftereffects of wartime malpractices can be. Thus we can have awareness. And we can act. The only proviso is that first we must have the will to do it. One can only hope that in this regard management will show greater wisdom this time than it often did last time. For if management does not make the great effort to protect the kind of economy we talk so much about, no one is going to protect it. We all know that the next five to ten years will tell that story.

Problems of Morale

Today mobilization for defense presents totally different problems of morale and psychology from those presented by mobilization in 1940 and 1941. In the days preceding our entry into the second World War there was no question in men's minds about the gigantic struggle in progress. There was a fear, almost a conviction, that we were bound to be drawn into it, and everyone—from top management to the plant sweeper—was convinced he had to do his part to help the country rearm for defense.

After Pearl Harbor, the need for coöperation and common purpose was evident to all, and the record shows what industry did in an all-out effort. Of course, there were mistakes, and those we must try to analyze so as not to repeat them; but the will and the unity were there in overwhelming measure, and with the American people there is no question of the old adage being true—that where there is a will, there is a way.

Today the greatest problem seems to be to fire them with this will. If we are to carry out the program that Charles E. Wilson has outlined, we have got to expand our industrial capacity. A long period of constant defense effort, superimposed on top of our normal scale of living, will spell increased output all along the line; and in the long run increased output is the only thing that is going to prevent ruinous inflation.

But today there is a discouraging lack of determination on the part of top management to authorize the necessary expansion. This is not true everywhere, of course. There are notable exceptions, and fortunately many of them are high in the ranks of industrial leadership. By and large, however, I get the impression that the feeling is: "Why should I bother about defense business? I have got all the civilian business I can handle. Let me keep my customers happy by giving them deliveries. I can even get the civilian business of the poor sap who has filled his plant with war work."

The usual motives which move businessmen to act are absent at the moment. There is not the patriotic fervor to defend the country. Indeed, there are real doubts whether adequate defense is needed. And certainly at the moment—thanks to price controls and excess profits taxes—there is no profit motive for expansion. The only motive really left to persuade a manufacturer to get into defense operation is fear of shortage of materials.

The morale problem, therefore, that members of American industry now face begins right with top management. Top management's first job is to get its own morale straightened out, to believe that industrial expansion and war work are an essential part of survival for America in general and for its own business in particular.

There are a great number of businesses everywhere in the country that have failed to make use of all the latest ways of increasing production. This is especially true in New England. At a recent meeting of certain federal procurement officials and New England businessmen the question was asked of one of the officials why New England was not getting its full share of war production business. This man put his finger on what I believe is the truth. He said, "You, here in New England, make the best machine tools in the world, but you ship them to other places and don't use them yourselves. Your costs are higher thereby."

The opportunity for new increased defense work is also an opportunity to get ourselves in shape for the future. It is a chance to experiment with new methods of control, manufacture, and engineering—a chance, in fact, to inject a new kind of thinking into our whole lower management staff. But, to repeat, we have got to get that new kind of thinking at the top first.

In normal times, even if we felt we could be assured of, say, twice our usual run of business for at least two or three years, I hope we would not just sit back with a sigh of relief. Of course, it would be a relief, but we should use such increased business to streamline everything in our manufacturing processes. Today that opportunity is being offered to us, and I believe, if it is put in such a light to our supervisory staffs—and particularly to our technical groups—and if those men are on their toes at all, that they will grab the ball and run with it farther than we can imagine. Pointing out this opportunity is our best sales tool in building up our organization to meet the defense challenge.

It gives us a sales tool, also, to use with our factory workers and with their leaders. The ranks of labor are inherently suspicious of all improved methods. Basically such attitudes among workers stem from the fear that improved methods will mean losing jobs. With regard to defense business, however, this fear can be removed. There will be increased payrolls, increased union members, increased employment, no matter how efficient we can become. In fact, improved efficiency is the only way to get all our possible share of defense work; there is not going to be enough available man power to get it otherwise. Again, increased efficiency is our best possible sales tool, because that is the way to insure continued employment when the defense effort is over. The unions have everything to gain by working with management to use the present opportunity for self-improvement.

Now, actually, what does all this mean in terms of personnel? Largely it means the same things we had to go through in the second World War. It means training at every level. We can think easily and quickly of the need for training the actual factory workers. Unskilled people have got to be brought up to become skilled, or at least semiskilled. Those problems we have gone through before, and we can go through them again.

The training of supervisors is certainly just as important. Foremen training should be a continuing process, and the training of new and additional foremen is the same old story, on a larger scale. Emphasis, however, should be placed continuously on the opportunity that increased production gives us to use new methods. Resourcefulness, imagination, administrative ability, and above all coöperation with staff technicians should be the theme.

The group who can perhaps do the most is the staff group. They need an indoctrination course to teach them that expansion for defense is not just doing more of the same. Let us all forget the word "same." The problem is to do *more,* and to find new ways of doing it so that we can do it with *less.* Methods men and engineers must take as much of the skill as they can out of the jobs in the factory, because more skilled people just are not available. Production control men must see that things move faster so that we can turn out more work with less inventory tied up.

Those who are engaged in production must not be satisfied with doing what has been done before. They must be encouraged, for example, to listen to salesmen who have new types of equipment to sell: "You never can lose, and you might gain a lot" should be the motto. Furthermore, if the new equipment is to be used for government work, there are always ways to finance it (the details are beyond the scope of this talk).

This is a mass-production country, but there are so many small businessmen who say, "Mass production is all right for the automobile people, but it doesn't apply to my business." I have had that feeling because I am in a business where a lot of twenty-five is considered a big lot, but we are finding that if we can increase our lots from twenty-five to fifty, there are quite a few mass-production techniques we can use which formerly we did not imagine were practical for us. That is the new kind of thinking that I believe we should use all down the line to stimulate morale.

Even in the best run businesses, I believe the opportunities that expanded war work give us can be made to pay off, not just now but in the future as well. This is a morale problem, but, again, it is a problem largely of the morale of top management. In my experience, staff people are constantly suggesting new ideas that are generally squelched. If top management will give the staff organization a chance to run with the ball and a little encouragement, the morale of these men will take care of itself, and then ingenuity will provide the increased production.

Of course, the staff and the supervisory group must be expanded. In achieving expansion, however, too much stress cannot be laid on picking administrative and executive character, rather than the best technician, to head the expansion program. In any technical job, of course, technical competence is essential; there are quantities of people with technical competence, however, and not so many with administrative ability. Imagination, resourcefulness, and, above all, the ability to get coöperation from others are just as essential in the technical department as anywhere else. The best salesman does not always make the best sales manager, just as the best workman does not necessarily make the best foreman. We must remember that in our technical work and make our selections on the basis of executive ability.

To sum this up, I think our greatest problem is getting top management to sell itself on the need to enter war production. Having sold itself on that, its next job is to sell itself on using war production as an opportunity to improve methods and techniques—not just in order to do the war work more cheaply, but to be in shape to do civilian work more cheaply when the emergency is over. Once it has sold itself on these things, it can then sell all the other groups on them. They all have everything to gain from the expansion, because it gives them an opportunity to improve their own positions—the workers to get greater security; the unions, more dues-paying members; the supervisors, greater opportunities; the staff and technical people, a real chance to cut costs materially, as well as to enjoy the rewards that come from doing that sort of work; and top management itself, the opportunity to maintain present profits through increased volume.

Problems of Communication

In the next year and a half, whether we are engaged in a "cold war," a "lukewarm war," or a "hot war," we are, for sure, going to be engaged in an all-out struggle for production. For we have resolved to rearm ourselves and to contribute to the rearming of our friends so that, if the worst comes, we shall not have to stand alone. This rearmament would not be an easy effort under any circumstances. But on top of it we have also resolved to maintain our civilian standard of living at as high a level as possible for as long as possible. Thus, we shall have a twofold production problem: (1) to *shift* some of our productive efforts from civilian to war production; (2) to *increase* our total effort so that we may have a fair amount of butter while, at the same time, we are making the guns—and guided missiles—called for by the program of preparedness. We are going to be mighty busy.

To get this program under way, and to sustain it—who knows for how long?—we shall, obviously, have to construct quantities of the most up-to-date production facilities and to employ our very best production and engineering techniques. We know from experience that we can do things of this sort at least as well as, if not better than, any other country. But, as we also know, production facilities and production techniques do not of themselves add up to production. Production also takes the *will* to produce; it takes teamwork or coöperation—call it what you will. Accordingly, while we are thinking about the problems of developing organizations for the coming struggle for production, it is entirely in order that we give some thought to the administrative problems of securing and maintaining the teamwork and coöperation which will be needed just as much as the best of facilities and the latest production techniques if we are to reach our goals.

Now, as we know, the morale and effectiveness of any team or group—whether a factory or air force squadron—depend on many things: on technical proficiency and training, on incentives and rewards, on ample opportunity for the individual to contribute to his utmost capacity, on the fact—as well as the feeling—of group solidarity and purpose, and on free and easy communication among the members of the group, just to name a few of the things which make for what we sometimes call teamwork.

It is about this last factor—communication—that I should like to say a few words. I should like to do so for two reasons: (1) because of the inherent importance of free and full communication for good teamwork in *any* circumstances; and (2) because of the great and special danger that communication may become *less* free and *less* full at the very time when we shall have a critical need for good teamwork.

Easy and complete communication throughout the organization seems invariably to be associated with good teamwork. In any group whatever, where morale and teamwork are high, we may be sure that there is a free and full interchange of facts, ideas, plans, wishes, preferences, feelings, and just plain fancies, among the members of that group. This idea turns up again and again in the studies of coöperation which have been made by members of the Harvard Business School faculty for the past quarter century. Our own common sense and experience as members of teams and working groups will bear out the findings of this clinical research.

Let me give a few homely illustrations of how free and full communication is related to good teamwork. If a group of us are to work together effectively, we must be able to report facts to one another. We must be able to offer ideas to each other on what we think needs to be done, or might be done, or can be done. We must be able to tell one another what we would like to do, what we plan to do. Things of this sort constitute a *minimum* level of communication for any kind of coöperative effort at all. Without such communication we can have no kind of integrated effort; we will be working at cross purposes; we will be pushing when we should be pulling.

Beyond and above this minimum level of communication for *any* kind of teamwork *at all,* there are other things about which we must communicate if we are going to have an organization which has *capacity for growth and change.* We must have an organization in which new and novel ideas can be spoken of, and can circulate; we must be able to tell one another of ideas, even "screwball" ideas, ideas which may in and of themselves be impractical or visionary or even shocking but which may contain the germ of something worth while. At first glance, probably, most new ideas, when they first break out of their shell, seem curious, if not startling or even repelling, to those who have not done the hatching themselves. But, if we do not give them at least a fair reception, we may stultify and discourage the offering of new ideas in the future. The team which is imaginative, which can see new angles, which can improvise on the spot, is one in which there is free circulation of ideas, in which even the most outlandish kind of a new idea can at the very least get a hearing and consideration before it is abandoned. The good team maintains, so to speak, a "free market" to which all kinds of ideas can come in search of a buyer, without being cut off at the source.

Beyond this, again, if we are to have a personally satisfying team to which we all feel a strong loyalty, and to which we offer our co-operation *spontaneously* because we *desire* to do so and obtain *pleasure* from doing so, there are other things about which we must be able to communicate. We must have freedom to communicate our personal, perhaps very personal feelings about things—how they are going, or how we wish they were going for us and for the group as a whole. We must be able to tell one another of our preferences—even whims and crotchets. For if we can speak of things of this sort, we shall be a team indeed, a closely bound group which can stick together when things are tough and the outlook none too bright.

Obviously, all of us on the team must take part in this process of communication. We cannot have some members left out in the cold. If the team is to remain a team and not break up, this process of communication cannot be restricted to a small elite circle. The ones who are left out will cease to be members. We will lose the benefit of their ideas and the strength of their loyalty.

If we are to have this full and free communication and good teamwork, if we are to have high morale, people must listen to us and pay some attention to what is on our minds. And in turn we must listen to them and pay attention to what is on their minds, too. Communication must flow without obstruction—up, down, sideways, back and forth—and to everyone in the group.

This goes not only for us, but for all individuals on all teams—directors, presidents, vice presidents, department heads, foremen, or the men—and women, too, don't forget—who work at the machines.

Having recalled the important relation between full and free communication and good teamwork, I should like now to suggest some of the special dangers which may threaten this process in the period ahead of us.

First, we are all of us going to be terribly busy and under all sorts of pressures to meet and beat schedules. This process of communication, we may come to say, just takes too much time—to explain to everybody, to listen to everybody. When we are up to our ears in work and our nerves are taut, working through to clear understandings and agreements may often seem to be the one more thing we just do not have time for.

Secondly, there is going to be a lot of milling around of the population as we shift to war production and take people into the armed forces. Many people who are not really accustomed to employment are going to be absorbed by industry. Consequently, most companies are going to have a turnover of personnel at all levels and are going to have a fair amount of "green" help. New people have to work into the team, to learn the ground rules and customs that the "old hands" know all about. This gives rise to an additional communication load. Often, because of the very fact that we think of them as "green" and inexperienced, we may be tempted to exclude them—on the ground that they would not understand or that they would not have anything worth while to say anyway—from the group to whom we explain things and to whom we look for ideas.

Again, all of us are going to have a lot on our minds. We are going to have friends and relatives in the armed forces. We shall be worrying about them. And we shall be worrying about Korea, Iran, Greece, or where-not, as well as about taxes, prices, controls, and shortages. We shall be in constant danger of being so preoccupied with our own worries and problems that we will not have time or energy to devote to those of others. And especially will this be true when *their* problems seem to us so trivial—or insoluble, in any event.

Moreover, many of us will be working under conditions where national security may prevent us from talking about certain matters, prevent us from explaining what we are doing and why. These potential blocks to communication would be bad enough if all they did was to reduce communication. But—as we also all know—"actions speak louder than words." If we fail to explain, if we fail to solicit ideas, if we fail to listen to ideas offered, if we fail to listen to what our people want us to know, our actions, if not our words, will communicate our attitude: "You people just aren't very important; we just aren't very much interested in you or your ideas." We all know full well what *that* communication will do to the teamwork we are trying to get.

Sometimes, when we feel ourselves moving in the direction of cutting short the communication process—especially the communication *up*—we might do worse than to recall a passage from General Eisenhower's *Crusade in Europe*. You will remember that he had a large organization, made up of a lot of "green" people, with lots of tough technical problems, critical time pressures, and soul-testing responsibilities. This is what he said:

> At times I received advice from friends, urging me to give up or curtail visits to troops. They correctly stated that, so far as the mass of men was concerned, I could never speak, personally, to more than a tiny percentage. They argued, therefore, that I was merely wearing myself out, without accomplishing anything significant, so far as the whole Army was concerned. With this I did not agree. In the first place I felt that through constant talking to enlisted men I gained accurate impressions of their state of mind. I talked to them about anything and everything: a favorite question of mine was to inquire whether the particular squad or platoon had figured out any new trick or gadget for use in

infantry fighting. I would talk about anything so long as I could get the soldier to talk to me in return.

I knew, of course, that news of a visit with even a few men in a division would soon spread throughout the unit. This, I felt, would encourage men to talk to their superiors, and this habit, I believe, promotes efficiency. There is, among the mass of individuals who carry the rifles in war, a great amount of ingenuity and initiative. If men can naturally and without restraint talk to their officers, the products of their resourcefulness become available to all. Moreover, out of the habit grows mutual confidence, a feeling of partnership that is the essence of *esprit de corps.*

If Eisenhower found it useful to take such pains in trying to keep communication free and full in *his* organization, maybe the rest of us can do the same in *our* organizations, despite the obstacles and pressures.

BUSINESS PROGRESS TOWARD STATESMANSHIP

Thomas D. Cabot, Horace N. Gilbert, Benjamin M. Selekman, George P. Baker, and Stanley F. Teele

Introduction

If statesmanship is defined merely as concern with affairs of state, there can be little doubt that business, particularly big business, is making progress in that direction. In the past twenty years, the growing regimentation of industry has led businessmen to take an increasing interest in national affairs. In 1932 through the NRA, in the second World War through the WPB and OPA, and today through the ODM, DPA, and OPS, hosts of businessmen have been brought to Washington to appear on both sides of the conference table. As a measure of the growth of businessmen's interest in national and international affairs, think of the growth of business associations devoted to discussion of various aspects of public policy.

But concern with affairs of state is not quite the same as statesmanship. The real question is: Has the interest in national affairs which has been forced on business caused businessmen to think more in terms of what is in the public interest and less in terms of what is in their own private interest? It seems to me that this, too, must be answered in the affirmative. A generation or two ago, business concerned itself almost wholly with the profit on individual transactions. No one would deny that it still concerns itself with profits, but today mere shrewd trading is rarely enough for success. Business has learned that in the long run the profits it keeps are

NOTE: Mr. Cabot is Director of National Security Affairs, United States Department of State; Mr. Gilbert is Professor of Business Economics, California Institute of Technology; Mr. Selekman is Kirstein Professor of Labor Relations, Harvard Business School; Mr. Baker is Professor of Transportation, Harvard Business School; Mr. Teele is Associate Dean and Professor of Business Administration, Harvard Business School.

The introduction is by Mr. Cabot; the sections on international relations and labor relations represent the observations of Mr. Gilbert and Mr. Selekman, respectively; the conclusion is drawn from the combined remarks of Mr. Baker and Mr. Teele.

to a considerable extent determined by the concern it shows for public welfare. Almost every head of a large business will testify that he is more anxious about the government "climate" in which his company must operate than he is about his sales staff's being able to continue to make profitable transactions. And most businessmen have learned that by constructive work with government agencies or by serious study of government policies they have the best opportunity to affect that climate, or, at least, to understand and live under it.

In international affairs, business has a great stake and is showing increasing interest. With our unique reservoir of capital there are immense opportunities for American business abroad, but it will take real statesmanship to make the most of these opportunities. The degree of coöperation and understanding which goes with the capital that is invested in any foreign venture can make the difference between success and failure.

The history of foreign investments is a record of many failures, most of which were due to lack of business statesmanship. It is the international, political, social, and economic problems, rather than ordinary business hazards, that have caused most losses. Those enterprises which have been managed with constant regard for the interests of *both* countries—the home of the enterprise and the home of the owner—have shown the most promise of prolonged success.

I answer, then, the question of progress toward statesmanship with an unqualified "yes," but as to whether the progress is fast enough I have some doubt. The world turns at an accelerating rate. The modern complexities of mass production have made individual effort and initiative a poor guarantee of security. Unless business can cope with the growing feeling of insecurity, it will not avoid further control by those who take their mandate from all the people.

It is a most difficult problem for business, indeed for all groups, to find a proper balance between security and freedom. In this country freedom was our heritage, and I join wholeheartedly with those who demand that freedom should be our legacy. Nevertheless, we must recognize that the degree of freedom permissible in pioneer days is not permissible today.

We must preserve the profit motive and the driving force of competition. Our policy of rewarding the efficient and rejecting the inefficient has spurred us to unparalleled productivity. But the policy of "devil take the hindmost" can be carried too far. To send back to the bench a businessman who fails to make a profit is a necessary process of weeding out those who waste labor and materials in producing goods the public does not value above cost; but to allow this process to deprive a man of his livelihood is a very different matter.

To preserve the enterprise system, to get a maximum of freedom with a satisfactory degree of security, will take a high order of statesmanship; and unless business contributes to this statesmanship, it is doomed.

Let us go on, now, to consider businessmen's progress toward statesmanship in two specific—and difficult—areas: international relations and labor relations.

In International Relations

The question of business's progress toward statesmanship in international relations has several facets, the most obvious of which probably are the attitudes of business toward trade and investment. I have decided not to deal with these sectors of the subject, but instead to present briefly a less obvious idea in the broad field of the progress American business is making in its attitude toward the relations between this country and the rest of the world. Germany afforded an excellent opportunity, during my recent eighteen months there with the High Commission, to observe and study the question of statesmanship at first hand.

The particular point I wish to present is this: There is a crying need in the rest of the world for the enterprise spirit and high-level business management competence that are so well developed in the United States. In fact I see little hope for the accomplishment of better living standards in the rest of the world unless the quality of business enterprise and management is raised. I do not belittle the good that has resulted from the huge gifts of money we have made since the end of the war, but I fear that the benefits will be short-lived. Even if Paul Hoffman's goal of an integrated Western European economy is attained, I fear that productivity will still remain seriously below that in the United States. The internal forces, in the countries with which I am familiar, which might possibly lead to an improvement of the quality of business enterprise and management, are not strong enough.

This then, is the challenge to the statesmanship of American business in its attitude toward the relations between the United States and the rest of the world that I wish to emphasize: the export of more of the enterprise and management talents developed to such a high degree in the United States and the application of those talents to the crying needs of the rest of the people that inhabit this troubled and suffering world. Such exports will not cost us the billions of dollars that programs such as the Marshall Plan cost; they even offer opportunities for financial profit.

American business is realistic, and to survive it has found that income must cover outlays. But American business is also idealistic, and the repeated proven miracle of many business experiences has been that great profit has attended bold idealistic ventures. It is even possible that the unique and highly developed form of business competition in this country will force American business to follow some such line as I am suggesting in the foreign field.

This idea is not new. American business covers the world, and it is contributing to the improvement of enterprise and management standards wherever it goes. I am simply arguing for more of the same thing. For the productivity of major sectors of the economies of countries with low living standards can be, and, indeed, *must* be raised. The United States has relied too much, I am afraid, on the idea that poverty can be bought off with money. Until a country has able enterprisers and high-level business managers, money gifts alone are liable to afford only a temporary illusion of well-being, and they may lead to dependency and bad feeling.

The record of American business experience abroad is interesting and contains many significant lessons. I was able to observe directly the operations of some concerns in Germany and in Western Europe that were controlled by us. At meetings in Paris of representatives from all ECA Missions favorable testimony was invariably given regarding the role played by United States interests in raising productivity.

In urging American business to assist with the raising of enterprise and high-level management standards in the foreign field, I am fully aware of the pitfalls that are almost certain to be encountered. The cynic can point to a selective record, and argue that we should stay at home. I agree that the situation must be reasonably propitious, and, especially important, that the top management of concerns undertaking such foreign operations must possess real qualities of statesmanship. The *concept* of United States standards regarding business enterprise and management competence is suited for export, but the *detailed applications* must be tailored to individual national circumstances. When we stress the importance of exporting our know-how, the question arises as to what progress has been made to foster an economic climate which will attract United States capital to Europe and just how to go about exporting our know-how.

To understand this problem, it is necessary to separate the supply function from the enterprise-management function. There are technical difficulties in foreign countries with respect to the possibility of future investment, while there are not such rigid limitations upon the flow of business know-how in enterprise.

It does require a tremendous amount of ingenuity to become established in certain countries, in certain situations. But Germany in particular could attract a capital investment program. Changes are being made every day there in the direction of greater normalcy. It is unnecessary for me to spell out the technicalities with respect to that status. The important thing is not the amount of capital involved in the deal, anyway.

I am not expecting any American company to put up a lot of capital in connection with my idea; I am stressing know-how. Of course, in most cases a little capital would have to go along with it, but also in most cases local capital could be found. In Western Europe, especially, there are several countries with some very good reservoirs of enterprise capital; Switzerland is the outstanding example.

The problem of where the capital comes from then is a secondary one. As for the question of how to export know-how, I have avoided spelling that out because there can be a myriad of forms. The important thing is that it be done. In my opinion the best way to do it is by example. That does not mean, however, that it should all be done by our groups going in as teams and actually taking over; the very fact that American companies are operating in a country gives to the country concerned a competitive norm against which to work.

I would say that the operating procedure of our top-name companies abroad is now more or less fixed; the tricks of the trade have been rather well learned. No American company operates abroad just as it does here. It has to adapt itself to circumstances, employ a good many local people, but it can add to local talents the essential differential—know-how—which distinguishes this country in such a notable fashion.

International Harvester, for example, is operating in Europe in an efficient manner, and yet, at the same time, it is attacking some problems that are basic to the economy of Western Europe. Westinghouse is also operating in several foreign countries and doing on its own a real American job. I am much impressed by its operations. We need more of this kind of thing.

There are, however, operations under contract where the identity of the American backer may be almost lost. But the contract can carry with it a specification with respect to the availability of know-how people on the top-management level. The important thing is that the level of competence be raised.

In this connection, I am reminded of an incident which Mr. Cabot has related to me. Here it is, in his own words:

> Cabot and Company was building a manufacturing plant in Liverpool. The first time I visited the plant under construction, I noticed a bunch of men chipping off the top foundation wall with coal chisels and hammers. I thought it slow and wondered why they did not use an air hammer. Then it occurred to me to wonder why they were chipping it off at all.

I asked the chief engineer, and he said that they had made a mistake and poured in an inch of concrete too high on the foundation part of the tower. We looked at the blueprint. It was only the louvers which shield the spray from being blown off. I asked him what the use of doing it was, since it only made a difference of an inch on the skyline, and that did not matter. He said it was not right. I argued with him half an hour trying to convince him. (The job was costing us over one thousand pounds sterling a day, and this was holding it up.)

I had to take the matter to the chairman of the board of construction before I could get anybody to agree it did not make any sense at all to be chipping off the top of the wall.

In looking at the United States from Europe during the period I spent there, I, too, was struck by the distinctive differential of management competence. We are, to put it one way, pouring the best of our young blood into the field of management competence. Europe has not done that. It has not done so, in many cases, because there is a kind of social stigma attached to this type of professional calling; but we can, by going abroad, in any one of many ways, raise the level of this know-how, and to my mind it is about the only way really to raise the standard of living of those European countries.

What of the relationship between American foreign policy and the operations of American concerns abroad? It almost goes without saying that the world is allergic to economic imperialism. The particular challenge I am making places no reliance on extraordinary aid from our State Department; such aid is an obsolete concept. American business must arrange for its own welcome and work out its own plans in accordance with existing laws and regulations or as amendments can be agreed upon.

Competitive relationships with local concerns do present, as I have stated, some of the most difficult problems. Often it is necessary to work through concerns which qualify as domestic. The resultant contribution, however, to the improvement of standards of business enterprise and high-level business management, whether direct or indirect, is an important means, in my opinion, to the increase of economic productivity, and thereby to the reduction of the injustices which are threatening the peace of the world.

In Labor Relations

If adjustment to shifts in power is a criterion of statesmanship, business, in my opinion, is making decided progress in that direction. I think this is all the more noteworthy because business is constantly faced with situations that cause more irritation, more tension, more annoyance, and more *daily* headaches than do even the precarious international relations and crises in Russia, Europe, or Asia. There are in labor relations also, of course, the phenomena of "crisis." But more continuously there are the frictions and the problems that arise between men who must—and want to—learn to live together. There is the picket line. There is the business agent of the union. There are the annual demands, and they have been pretty substantial demands of late. The way a business meets these situations—which are compounded of historic ingredients, but now in such changed proportions that the mix seems new—measures whether it is making progress toward statesmanship in this area of collective bargaining.

And just here lies the nub of today's problems in labor relations. The challenge to management arises from a development the very nature of which most of us have yet to recognize. A new power equation has formed in industry, and the real job before management is nothing less than adaptation to a potent new power group. Everyone dealing with economic affairs in business is constantly being challenged by other people. Many groups—and certainly the union representatives, always seeking a foothold in industry—may have been challenging before, but, in recent years, they have acquired power to make their challenge stick.

The significant characteristic about the new equation that they have thus been forming in the economy is that each powerful element in it depends on all the others. It is impossible to introduce a minus sign; no single integer can eliminate another, as we all have been learning from experience abroad, without changing the fundamental character of the equation itself. To put the job in simple mathematical terms, we in the United States must find the working answers that will make *Big Business* + *Big Unionism* + *Big Government* = *Modern Democracy.*

Our labor movement—the young CIO and the rejuvenated AFL, as well as a miscellany of independent unions—has introduced the new counter into this equation. It is organized fifteen million strong; it has, for the first time in our history, secure positions in mass-production industries. It has militant leaders, not modest, not bashful, willing to call a spade a spade, willing to make demands—and call strikes to enforce these demands. John L. Lewis is only the most dramatic example of labor's new men of power; he is certainly not the only one.

Now, have businessmen, have all of us, indeed, made progress, first, in understanding that new power equation and, secondly, in adapting ourselves to it effectively and realistically? Can business seek both profit and statesmanship? Can it combine its continuing production services to the community with novel social adjustments that will gradually ameliorate the raw aspects of this power situation, and so help to transmute the relationships between organized interest groups, ever poised for potential conflict, into something more accountable, more workable, more viable, than the recurrent recourse to naked power clashes?

Even when the goal is set so high, I think we can feel that we are making considerable progress. Many of us do not realize how steadily we have been moving ahead on significant new trails. The seemingly endless appearance of fresh hurdles that we must clear along this still uncertain road ahead understandably narrows perspective. We grow so discouraged with yesterday's walkout by labor in Washington, with today's demand for an improvement factor in wages, with tomorrow's threat from the ties between living costs and wage rates, that we do not really get the pleasure and satisfaction of seeing how good a job we have already done. Moreover, even if we have not welcomed that job, even if we have not tackled it with relish, we *have* tackled it. Accomplishments have come to us by the practical common sense, the American know-how, of adjusting one's self to inescapable reality.

I direct your attention to two dates to indicate the progress we have made: 1937 and, over a decade later, 1950. There was no labor movement to speak of in this country up until about 1937. In 1930, there were marginal unions in the building trades, in the railroads, in coal mining, in the needle trades, and so on. But there were no unions in steel, in rubber, in electrical manufacturing, in agricultural machinery manufacturing, in oil, in chemicals—or, in a word, anywhere in the whole long list of basic, mass-production industries.

Then, in 1937, the Wagner Act was validated. It was passed in 1935, but did not really go into effect until the Supreme Court declared it constitutional in 1937. Things began to happen—suddenly.

That year of upheaval, 1937, resounded with the challenge of the sit-down strikes. They swept the automobile industry after mounting to an early and most dramatic climax at Flint, when the automobile workers seized the General Motors plants. They barricaded themselves behind the doors and kept management and the foremen out. They held on to that property until Mr. Knudsen, representing General Motors, informed Governor Murphy of the "recognition" settlement that had been worked out with union representatives led by John L. Lewis. This agreement gave the union its first contractual rights to bargain with General Motors.

That was also the year of the Little Steel strike. For over a month "industrial warfare" pitted local police, strikers, and company forces against one another as violence erupted in many steel communities —raw violence at South Chicago, the so-called Chicago Massacre, where some fifty people, policemen and strikers, were killed.

Now, let us turn to 1950 and, again, look at General Motors. Whereas the workers won their first agreement in 1937 by a seizure of the property, which showed bitter, almost irreconcilable conflict, when General Motors initialed its third post-war agreement with the UAW in 1950, it was setting pioneering patterns for peace in basic industry, especially in the automobile and allied industries.

Perhaps even more significant than the terms of that agreement is the way it came about. The beginnings were registered in the 1948 contract. General Motors had "taken a strike" after the war that lasted five months. Why? What did the workers really want that made them act this way? Mr. Wilson, the president of General

Motors, got to thinking about this when he was hospitalized after a skating accident. He decided to investigate.

The workers wanted a guarantee that their earnings would stay fairly stable. They wanted also some sort of guarantee that their standard of living would improve as productivity increased.

Mr. Wilson told himself that these were perfectly sound aspirations. Did not management really want employees to have these same things? But, then, was not there some orderly way to work this all out without having a new schedule of "wants" thrown at management every year or two with all the attendant wrangling, and, so often, with resort to power? If General Motors was as good as it was supposed to be in turning out cars and gadgets and Diesels, why could it not manage to meet this test of good production, too? So Mr. Wilson called in the staff members of the corporation and asked them to think through a program which would satisfy these reasonable, persisting employee demands in some reasonable, continuing way. A three-pronged formula resulted:

(1) The employees were offered the contractual guarantee that they would be able to buy as much with an hour's pay as they could in 1940.

(2) Since productivity had been going up some 2 per cent a year throughout the country, a corresponding automatic increase in the hourly rate was projected. At the same time the union and company workers had to agree—and this was to be spelled out in the contract—that only through having the freedom to introduce modern technology and labor-saving devices would the corporation be able to attain the objective of continually rising productivity.

(3) In return, the corporation asked to be guaranteed a certain measure of stability in costs and relationships through a long-term contract.

It takes courage to ask an organization with over one million members and a very militant leadership to forego the opportunity of using its pressure and its strike power for five years. It takes courage also for a union to agree. But General Motors put its points across, and—by 1950—the parties translated their "wage formula" into a five-year contract.

Incidentally, I am not going into the arguments concerning the inflationary potential of this "GM formula." It is not fair, however, to accuse General Motors or the UAW of being responsible for inflationary pressures because of the escalator principle and the improvement factor that were incorporated into their basic wage settlement. That contract formula was projected and tested in the normal development of collective bargaining procedures before anyone had any idea that the Korean aggression would break upon us.

Indeed, the fundamental importance of such pioneering experiments in collective bargaining stems, let us say once again, from their underlying recognition that this country today manages its affairs through three great types of organizations: corporations, unions, and political parties. These are the units in the controlling power equation; and the sooner we face up to all its implications, the better will be our chances for working out its solution. The fact that General Motors has been able, in a thirteen-year span, to evolve from a situation of opposed raw power to one of working relationships under a negotiated treaty of accommodation, I count among the outstanding achievements in the business history—yes, and in the social history—of this country. It affords a dramatic example of that kind of evolution toward statesmanship upon which so much depends for our whole national future.

Let us look at another such example of progress, which was similarly achieved through one of the prime procedures of collective bargaining, through contract negotiation, at the Ford Motor Company. In 1945, at the conclusion of the war, Ford felt that management had not been getting a "fair return" upon its first investments in good relations under the union agreement. Many difficulties required straightening out. Particularly disturbing had been the constant undisciplined recourse to wildcat strikes. Despite the agreement which stipulated that there should not be any stoppages while the contract was in effect, and despite the establishment of adequate grievance machinery, including arbitration, department after department, group after group, walked out to protest shop complaints.

Thus it was that, when the time arrived to open negotiations on the first post-war contract in 1945–1946, the company had given careful preliminary thought to its strategy. Its first communications to the union established a position something like this:

> You have presented to us many far-reaching demands. You want a 30 per cent increase in wages; you want everybody to have straight seniority; you want to help us decide on productivity standards; and so on. But we will not discuss a single thing until some formula is worked out for eliminating wildcat strikes. In order to be productive, we have to have discipline.

Proposals, counterproposals, and counter-counterproposals followed. I will not go into details. Suffice it to say, the union finally agreed with the company that a formula must be worked out for effective curbs on illegal stoppages. Having got that close, the union leaders found a way to do it. In Article V of their new agreement, revealingly titled "Union Responsibility," they carefully defined "illegitimate strikes," established the procedures for mutual action upon them, and set forth the penalties for leadership and participation in them. The epidemic of wildcat stoppages virtually disappeared. Though disturbances still occur from time to time, as they always will in any large organization made up of emotional human beings working together, they have been predominantly small-scale and subject to orderly resolution.

Let me point out just what such case examples suggest regarding the progress that was registered through these epochal years since 1937 in the technique (or philosophy) of making agreements. Management at the outset seemed too often amateurish and on the defensive across the table from union spokesmen. The union took the offensive, management braced to resist—and company spokesmen usually lost if not more vital things, at least their tempers, somewhere in the give-and-take of the bargaining sessions. Now management comes in well prepared with a list of essentials that it thinks the corporation ought to have for the proposed duration of the agreement, and with objective data and economic reasons to support its demands. In other words, management really takes negotiation as negotiation: bargaining is bargaining; it balances demands and counterdemands; both sides have a right to present fair proposals. Less and less often is it the union only that makes demands. Increasingly now, management is abandoning the former nervously defensive attitude. Despite the context of full employment, ways are sought both to straighten out things which had proved themselves "wrong" under the past agreement and to build constructively and positively for the future.

Thus, management has taken seriously this matter of negotiating a contract, has applied to it good American common sense and, I think, good statesmanship. And thus collective negotiation becomes an instrument of accommodation, a way to preserve the effectiveness of business by reducing intrinsic power relationships to order and responsibility.

Another indication of our progress in this surcharged area of shifting power relations in the economy lies in management's approaches to the practices of arbitration. Before the 1930's, very few companies were willing to call in an arbitrator from "outside." They were afraid of what such "interventions" might portend in increased labor costs. They looked askance at judgments upon shop problems by men "who had probably never had to meet a payroll." Unquestionably arbitration decisions do often involve large sums of money. In any event, arbitration had simply failed to sink any widespread continuing roots in industry in those days. Only in the needle trades had the procedure attained any prestige, after the then "new" unionists succeeded in persuading Hart Schaffner & Marx in 1911 that voluntary arbitration represented the better way of resolving difficulties in industry—by "constitutionalism" rather than by walkouts and undisciplined behavior.

Today, however, there are very few business concerns that do not accept arbitration. I am not saying they are all happy about it. I am afraid corporations are not altogether happy about unions either. But the test of statesmanship lies, above all, in facing realistically and effectively those situations about which we are not happy! That is an integral part of statesmanship. To cull a clarifying example from an area fortunately far different from domestic industrial relations, we may at least concede that we are not exactly happy about Russia either! But we are facing up to the fact that Russia is going to be a part of the shrinking world as long as we are. From that reality, we proceed to the adjustment required by the facts we face, and strive to put ourselves in a position of power too, so that Russia will realize she cannot push us off the globe.

If, then, management now accepts arbitration too under this same type of compulsion, it is also converting this procedure of collective relations, like negotiation, into an instrument of ordered adjustment to new power realities. In utilizing arbitration procedures, again as in negotiation, business seeks to do a steadily better job. When I first started in arbitration work twenty-five years ago, I was always sorry for the businessmen. In the trades where they were arbitrating issues under union agreements, the labor people often seemed to make monkeys out of them. Certainly nothing like this is true any more. Today most companies have taken on good staffs, college-trained, business-school-trained, law-school-trained staffs; and they have put them in full-time charge of handling arbitration matters.

Whereas, formerly, I would say on the basis of my own experience, 75 per cent of arbiters' decisions went for labor, the proportion has probably been just about reversed today.

This is understandable. Not only are most corporations doing a better job of preparation, of standing up and presenting their cases, but also the intrinsic merits of their cases are usually better, for the simple reason that they take a contract more seriously than the union or the workers do. Remember, the union is a political organization. The rank-and-file workers always have a voice, and, if they say at a union meeting, "We want you to go to arbitration," even Mr. Reuther has to take the matter to arbitration—and even when a seasoned union official may deem the case contractually "weak."

By contrast, in most corporations every foreman is instructed to live up to the contract 100 per cent. As a matter of fact, many corporations—and, interestingly enough, particularly some of the "big" ones—have used the arbitration machinery to introduce that same positive component of statesmanship into those new power relations of which we have been here talking. I cannot think of anything more educative and maturing than having the parties thrash out the meaning of an agreement or of a contract clause in the presence of a neutral outsider.

After all, a labor contract is itself fundamentally one way of containing power—of ordering the relations between the organized interest groups, so that their respective power does not spill over into tugs of war. We want law, and in the labor contract the law is spelled out: what the power of management should be; what the rights of the workers are; and how daily problems of adjustment shall be adjudicated. Most contracts, in their early stages, are introduced into a plant by a situation of very raw compulsion; and the workers or unions are not accustomed to reading the contracts carefully. Their rights are protected. But they may want to go beyond their rights, and the contract sets a boundary against such encroachments.

Thus it is that corporate business is not only accepting the arbitration machinery but also making constructive use of it. Let me give you an illustration.

Suppose the businessman says, "Mr. Arbiter, we challenge your authority to hear this case. It is untimely by the procedural requirements of the contract. The appeal was made two weeks [let us say] rather than ten days after the final joint meeting on this grievance." (Contracts containing an arbitration clause provide that the appeal for arbitration must be made within a time limit.)

That may appear to be a highly legalistic approach—but it is not unusual. But legalisms, too, can be educative and influential. For example, the arbitrator may find means in this case to remind the corporation and its lawyers that they are not enforcing a commercial agreement, that they are dealing with "aggrieved" human beings who ask to have their day in court. Even though the final decision is likely to go for the corporation on the technicality of untimeliness, it may be desirable to give the union a hearing. If the workers are "heated" about the issue, this will drain off their excitement in an orderly way; otherwise the union officials might have a hard time keeping them in line. At the same time, the workers will have learned something about the binding nature of the contract.

At the opposite pole from arbitration looms the strike. Must strikes remain the criteria of failures in statesmanship? I do not think so. Indeed, it is itself revealing evidence of the progress I am here pin-pointing that strike experience too registers some of our most impressive markers of advance. I myself grew up in the coal and iron regions of Westmoreland County—in an atmosphere of strikes. They were terrible—violence and bloodshed. This was particularly true in the heavy industry of those years, as we children of Pennsylvania were observing it. But the last "old-model" steel strike was in 1937; and, although in 1946 and 1949 steel strikes occurred, they saw hardly a single act of violence. After all, the decisions on whether or not to call (or "take") a strike belong to the strategy of bargaining; the conduct of the resort to power and the manner of the settlement can partake of statesmanship.

Thus, in adjusting themselves to the power situation, the steel corporations (among others) have been manifestly deciding that, when the union calls a strike, the thing to do is to shut down the mills in an orderly way. They ask consent to have supervisors carry out certain strategic shutdown functions that will safeguard the very costly operating equipment, for example, to cool the hearths gradually, to turn off the boilers and gas, and so on; and the union usually agrees.

What is more, the management realizes that these very men who are striking are coming back to work. It would be ridiculous to try to starve people out! Management must be able therefore to resume operations with as good a feeling and as good a relationship as possible. Orders are piling up. In what spirit, then, will employees come back to work? In post-war strikes, steel companies even have sent out containers of hot coffee and sandwiches in winter weather to the picket line! Again, when the men on another occasion were "out" during the World Series, at least one company put up loudspeakers to broadcast the games to the men on the picket lines. That is statesmanship!

Does not labor also have the responsibility to acquire statesmanship, and is it making progress in that direction? Anybody who exercises power, nationally or internationally, has the responsibility to acquire statesmanship. Unless power is used constructively, in a statesmanlike way, the result is anarchy and immorality. Men, of course, like William Green, Walter Reuther, Philip Murray, and even John L. Lewis, would claim that they have been exercising quite a degree of statesmanship.

That may sound surprising. But they would go on to point out, as they have to me, that they could not get a hearing until they used power, until they got government on their side. And that is the truth.

In the old days, the typical behavior of the businessman, after an organizing campaign when he received a letter from a labor official saying, "I would like to meet with you; the workers have asked us [the union] to talk with you about negotiating an agreement," was to throw the letter in the wastebasket and not even answer it.

In the not too distant past, there was unemployment, serious unemployment. There was destitution. And, despite our marvelous productivity and our rising standard of living, the individual worker was often beset by insecurity and by the slighting of his status as a human being. The labor leaders claim that it was they who came in and forced industries to negotiate agreements. "We are getting a living wage, a higher standard of living for the worker," they say. "We are making businessmen think about productivity."

John L. Lewis takes credit for the tremendous rate of mechanization in the coal mines of his industry. He points out what is "really" wrong in Great Britain: her worries over coal now testify simply that management has been asleep there! The differences from the situation in this country, he says, can be traced preëminently to the fact that our union miners put so much pressure on management, to make it face social responsibilities and high wages, that it had to mechanize. There is hardly a single session in conventions of the United Mine Workers union at which he does not reiterate that claim.

Sidney Hillman, too, or one of his successors, would tell you the story of the sweatshop garment industry—uncontrolled competition, which resulted in long hours, low wages, crowded tenements, high rates of tuberculosis and other diseases. Neither management nor workers were satisfied. You could buy a suit for eight dollars, but, as they put it dramatically, the blood of the worker was woven in it.

There is no question but that the labor leaders have a case when they say that they faced up to social questions and were able to achieve a fair deal for the workingman only through power. Unfortunately, having achieved that power and having righted a lot of wrongs, too many of them still talk the underdog language of the old days, using words like *exploitation* and *Wall Street.* They have not yet achieved that adaptation to the whole changing economy as we would like them to.

The significant question, here, however, remains whether business has *more* responsibility for statesmanship than labor? I would say yes! Since I have been applying political terms to other aspects of the problem of power, I might compare management to His Majesty's Government, in the total job of production, and labor to His Majesty's opposition. The government of the day always has the first responsibility for positive policy; the opposition provides the needling that is essential to prevent lethargy and smugness.

This is a period of transition. I have found that, at least where businessmen are sincerely trying to move from the raw power struggle toward a more logical, more constructive, program—a program of statesmanship, if you will—despite all the pulling and hauling, the haggling, and, sometimes, even the threats of and resort to overt power, labor men will essentially "come along" too. In this transition, clearly, labor remains the power group which is seizing new positions in industrial relations; management, as the established power, must accomplish the major accommodations. The quality of our total adjustment can be determined, accordingly, by how business assimilates the new realities.

Please understand that I do not mean by all this that unions should be given everything they ask for. Quite the opposite. Accommodation is something very different from appeasement. The kind of statesmanship I have been describing pursues the orderly resolution of genuine conflicts in interests, of demands and counterdemands, by seeking always the maximum mutual benefit of those involved.

Let me conclude by making one plea. We talk about employee morale a great deal. I want to start a crusade for management and supervisor morale—for giving "a break" to the men who have to carry such crucial, focal responsibilities. They are crushed by overwork. They are under pressure from all sides. They get very little credit for what they are doing. Statesmanship requires leisure, time for thinking and trying to see where you are. Unfortunately, the only such leisure we usually get is the enforced kind, like Mr. Wilson's hospitalization—it is surprising how much good thinking has been done in hospitals!

Further, I believe that, if management realized the meaning of these new power situations, it would recover its zest. The wonderful thing about the management men I knew before the 1930's was that they had zest. They got pleasure out of coming to the office, doing things, accomplishing things. True, in previous generations, management never had the baffling problems it faces now; things were freer. But it seems to me that, because the challenges posed by these new power situations now loom greater, the satisfaction in meeting them should also be greater. There is fun in negotiating an agreement. In fact, the man who does not get fun out of negotiating a sound deal, in devising those "social inventions" that fit relations between the contracting parties to changing circumstances, should not go to the bargaining conference; he will not be good at it! Such men, moreover, will not make effective bargainers. There is pleasure in trying to plan your tactics and strategy, in facing a good opponent and slugging it out with him in a determined but understanding way, and in winning a good agreement. It is good statesmanship, too.

Conclusion

Statesmanship involves very hard work, far more than simply being a man of distinction who is a capable exalter by cliché. It involves seeing the forest despite the trees, being willing to look for the real reasons whenever your business or your industry is in a jam. And it involves being open-minded to all the various alternative courses of action which are suggested as a means of getting out of the various jams you are in or that you see coming upon you.

I think that this is the one thing I would list as the most difficult: being open-minded in regard to the viewpoints of those who violently differ with you and who feel they would gain by courses of action which you feel would hurt you. If men are going to get anywhere in working out common programs, I think that that is the heart of statesmanship, even though it involves a degree of compromise which is very distasteful to many men.

I have never forgotten a play I saw when I was a boy—*Strife,* a short play by John Galsworthy. It portrays a strong-minded labor leader and a strong-minded businessman. They held straight to their deeply ingrained principles and went down in complete collapse, both of them, at the end of the play, when more moderately-minded people got together on a program which we now would think was a conservative one. Obviously, the need was for statesmanship of the kind described by Professor Selekman.

I know some will feel that everything Professor Selekman recounted, except Mr. Wilson's hospitalization, proves that management has never used statesmanship except as forced by power demonstrations. But think a minute. What he said really proves the opposite. Major changes, such as we certainly have had during the last twenty years, do not come about easily. They do not come about without grief and pain. Admittedly, it would have been wonderful if the management groups had foreseen all developments and had moved somehow voluntarily in anticipation of them. But is not that an unrealistic expectation of the course of human affairs? And is not real statesmanship reflected primarily in adaptation, in the ability to adapt to what is happening, to reconcile the individual enterprise and the forces outside?

In situations where businessmen deal with each other's problems, there too statesmanship is required. The actual interests of the businessmen involved often vary widely. The broader-minded man realizes that fact to be true and realizes it is essential that they get together and work out some statesmanlike approach, whereby they can settle some of their own problems and keep the government from further and further controlling business.

In general, this requires compromise, and one of the greatest difficulties is for one man to admit he must give way from a strongly held principle. Often it involves giving way within himself as well as in his business.

There are many men who, because of the need of keeping balance within themselves, feel they must hold to a particular principle in their individual businesses. Even for the more flexible man, this makes the problem of being open-minded, in order to compromise, a difficult enough one. The real leader can rise above those internal difficulties, though they tend to be deep-rooted and very difficult to handle.

Let me close this chapter—and the book—with this observation: We do not want to be smug or self-satisfied. But maybe the observations made here ought to offset somewhat the tendency, which I notice among business groups, to wear sackcloth and ashes constantly, to belabor themselves with the notion that "there are so many things we should do, and we have not done very much." Real progress toward statesmanship *has* been made by business. Let us take what we have accomplished as a token of the progress which business can make in the future toward even greater statesmanship.

SUPPLEMENT

THINKING AHEAD FOR BUSINESS—A SELECTED BIBLIOGRAPHY

A SELECTED BIBLIOGRAPHY

Prepared by the Reference Department, Baker Library, Harvard Graduate School of Business Administration.

THE WORLD SITUATION AND AMERICAN ECONOMIC POLICY

Brookings Institution, International Studies Group, *Major Problems of United States Foreign Policy 1950–1951* (Washington, 1951), 416 pp.

Buchanan, Norman S., and Friedrich A. Lutz, *Rebuilding the World Economy; America's Role in Foreign Trade and Investment* (New York: Twentieth Century Fund, 1947), 434 pp.

Espy, Willard R., *Bold New Program* (New York: Harper & Brothers, 1950), 273 pp.

Franck, Peter G., and Dorothea Seelye Franck, "Implementation of United Nations Technical Assistance Programs," in *International Conciliation,* no. 468 (February 1951), pp. 61–80.

Gray, Gordon, *Report to the President on Foreign Economic Policies* (Washington: U. S. Government Printing Office, 1950), 131 pp.

Harris, Seymour E., ed., *Foreign Economic Policy for the United States* (Cambridge: Harvard University Press, 1948), 490 pp.

Hoffman, Paul G., *Peace Can Be Won* (New York: Doubleday, Doran & Company, Inc., 1951), 118 pp.

Hoskins, Halford L., ed., "Aiding Underdeveloped Areas Abroad," in *Annals of the American Academy of Political and Social Science,* 268 (March 1950), pp. 1–187.

Lewis, Cleona, *The United States and Foreign Investment Problems* (Washington: The Brookings Institution, 1948), 359 pp.

Patterson, Ernest Minor, ed., "Formulating a Point Four Program," in *Annals of the American Academy of Political and Social Science,* 270 (July 1950), pp. 1–149.

United Nations, Department of Economic Affairs, *World Economic Report, 1949–50* (New York: 1951), 247 pp.

U. S. Department of State, *Point Four; Cooperative Program for Aid in the Development of Economically Underdeveloped Areas* (Washington: U. S. Government Printing Office, January 1950), 167 pp. (Pub. 3719, Economic Cooperation Series 24)

U. S. International Development Advisory Board, *Partners in Progress; A Report to the President,* Nelson A. Rockefeller, Chairman (Washington: U. S. Government Printing Office, 1951), 120 pp.

"The United States in the World; Twentieth Anniversary Issue," in *Fortune,* XLI, no. 2 (February 1950)

Ward, Barbara, *Policy for the West* (New York: W. W. Norton & Company, Inc., 1951), 317 pp.

CENTRAL AND SOUTH AMERICA

Behrendt, Richard F., *Inter-American Economic Relations; Problems and Prospects* (New York: Carnegie Endowment for International Peace, 1948), 98 pp.

Gordon, Wendell Chaffe, *The Economy of Latin America* (New York: Columbia University Press, 1950), 434 pp.

Herring, Hubert Clinton, *Good Neighbors* (New Haven: Yale University Press, 1941), 381 pp.

Horn, Paul V., and Hubert E. Bice, *Latin-American Trade and Economics* (New York: Prentice-Hall, Inc., 1949), 682 pp.

International Bank for Reconstruction and Development, *The Basis of a Development Program for Colombia; Report of a Mission Headed by Lauchlin Currie and Sponsored by the International Bank for Reconstruction and Development in Collaboration with the Government of Colombia* [with summary] (Washington: U. S. Government Printing Office, 1950), 642 pp. (IBRD Special Pub. No. 1950.2). The summary also published separately. 76 pp. (IBRD Special Pub. No. 1950.1)

Miller, Edward G., Jr., "Economic Aspects of Inter-American Relations," in *Department of State Bulletin*, XXIII, no. 599 (December 25, 1950), pp. 1011–1016.

Perkins, Dexter, *United States and the Caribbean* (Cambridge: Harvard University Press, 1947), 253 pp. (American Foreign Policy Library)

U. S. Department of State, Office of Public Affairs, Division of Publications, *Report of the Joint Brazil-United States Technical Commission* (Washington, June 1949), 321 pp. (Pub. 3487.) A summary of the report was published in *Federal Reserve Bulletin*, XXXV, no. 4 (April 1949), pp. 361–373.

Whitaker, Arthur P., *The United States and South America; The Northern Republics* (Cambridge: Harvard University Press, 1948), 280 pp. (American Foreign Policy Library)

Wythe, George, *Industry in Latin America* (New York: Columbia University Press, 1949), 387 pp.

Wythe, George, et al., *Brazil: an Expanding Economy* (New York: Twentieth Century Fund, 1950), 412 pp.

EUROPE AND THE NEAR EAST

Alpert, Paul, *Twentieth Century Economic History of Europe* (New York: Henry Schuman, Inc., 1951), 466 pp.

Brookings Institution, The International Studies Group, "The Problem of European Integration," in its *Major Problems of United States Foreign Policy 1949–1950* (Washington, 1950), part III, no. 3, pp. 403–472).

Carey, Jane Perry Clark, "Western European Union and the Atlantic Community," in *Foreign Policy Reports*, XXVI, no. 7 (June 15, 1950), pp. 66–80.

Dean, Vera Micheles, *Europe and the United States* (New York: Alfred A. Knopf, 1950), 349 pp.

Ellis, Howard S., *The Economics of Freedom; The Progress and Future of Aid to Europe* (New York: Published for the Council on Foreign Relations by Harper & Brothers, 1950), 549 pp.

Gary, Howard C., "The U.S.S.R. Economic Strengths and Weaknesses," in *Foreign Policy Reports,* XXVII, no. 2 (April 1, 1951), pp. 14–23.

Krout, John A., ed., "The American Foreign Aid Program," *Proceedings of the Academy of Political Science,* XXIII, no. 4 (January 1950), 122 pp.

Margold, Stella K., "Economic Life in Russia's Orbit," in *Harvard Business Review,* XXVIII, no. 5 (September 1950), pp. 65–78; XXVIII, no. 6 (November 1950), pp. 86–113.

Organization for European Economic Cooperation, *European Recovery Programme; Second Report of the O.E.E.C.* (Paris, 1950), 281 pp.

Roucek, Joseph S., ed., "Moscow's European Satellites," in *Annals of the American Academy of Political and Social Science,* 271 (September 1950), pp. 1–184.

Royal Institute of International Affairs, *The Middle East; A Political and Economic Survey* (London, 1950), 496 pp.

Speiser, Ephraim A., *United States and the Near East,* rev. ed. (Cambridge: Harvard University Press, 1950), 283 pp. (American Foreign Policy Library)

United Nations, Economic and Social Council, Economic Commission for Europe, *Economic Survey of Europe in 1949* (Geneva: Department of Economic Affairs, 1950), 299 pp. (Pub. 1950.II.E.1)

U. S. Economic Cooperation Administration, *Report to Congress* (Washington: U. S. Government Printing Office, 1948 to date)

ASIA

Commonwealth Consultative Committee, *The Colombo Plan for Co-operative Economic Development in South and South-East Asia* (London: H.M. Stationery Office, 1950), 101 pp. (CMD 8080). An illustrated summary also published with title "New Horizons in the East" (London, H.M. Stationery Office, 1950), 40 pp.

Fairbank, John King, et al., *Next Step in Asia* (Cambridge: Harvard University Press, 1949), 90 pp.

Fairbank, John King, *United States and China* (Cambridge: Harvard University Press, 1948), 384 pp. (American Foreign Policy Library)

Jacoby, Erich H., *Agrarian Unrest in Southeast Asia* (New York: Columbia University Press, 1949), 287 pp.

Miller, Raymond W., "Our Economic Policy in Asia," in *Harvard Business Review,* XXIX, no. 4 (July 1951), pp. 52–70.

Mills, Lennox A. and Associates, *The New World of Southeast Asia* (Minneapolis: University of Minnesota Press, 1949), 445 pp.

Patterson, E. M., ed., "Lessons from Asia," *Annals of the American Academy of Political and Social Science,* 276 (July 1951), pp. 1–117.

Reischauer, Edwin O., *Toward a Far Eastern Policy* (New York: Foreign Policy Association, 1950), 61 pp. (Headline Series 84)

Reischauer, Edwin O., *The United States and Japan* (Cambridge: Harvard University Press, 1950), 357 pp. (American Foreign Policy Library)

Rosinger, L. K., et al., *The State of Asia, a Contemporary Survey;* under the auspices of the American Institute of Pacific Relations (New York: Alfred A. Knopf, Inc., 1951), 558 pp.

Thorner, Daniel, "Prospects for Economic Development in Southern Asia," in *Foreign Policy Reports,* XXVI, no. 3 (April 15, 1950), pp. 18–28.

United Nations, Economic and Social Council, Economic Commission for Asia and the Far East, *Economic Survey of Asia and the Far East,* 1949 (Lake Success: Department of Economic Affairs, 1950), 485 pp. (Pub. 1950.II.F.1)

U. S. Economic Survey Mission to the Philippines, *Report to the President of the United States by the Economic Survey Mission to the Philippines* [Daniel W. Bell, Chairman] (Washington: U. S. Government Printing Office, 1950), 107 pp.

Winfield, Gerald F., *China, the Land and the People* (New York: William Sloane Associates, in coöperation with the American Institute of Pacific Relations, 1948), 437 pp.

Wiser, Charlotte Viall and William H. Wiser, *Behind Mud Walls* (New York: Richard R. Smith, Inc., 1930), 180 pp.

COMMUNISM: THEORY AND PRACTICE

Armstrong, Hamilton Fish, *Tito and Goliath* (New York: The Macmillan Company, 1951), 226 pp.

Barghoorn, Frederick C., *The Soviet Image of the United States; A Study in Distortion* (New York: Harcourt Brace and Company, 1950), 297 pp.

Burnham, James, *The Coming Defeat of Communism* (New York: John Day, 1949), 248 pp.

Crossman, Richard H. S., ed., *The God That Failed; A Testament of Six Former Admirers of Communism* (New York: Harper & Brothers, 1949), 273 pp.

Hunt, Robert N. Carew, *The Theory and Practice of Communism* (London: Geoffrey Bles, 1950), 211 pp.

Malik, Charles, *The Challenge of Communism; An Address Delivered Before the Chicago Council on Foreign Relations, December 14, 1950* (Chicago: The Council, 1951), 12 pp.

Schlesinger, Arthur M., Jr., *What About Communism?* (New York: Public Affairs Press, 1950), 32 pp. (Public Affairs Pam. 164)

U. S. Congress, House, Committee on Foreign Affairs, *The Strategy and Tactics of World Communism; Report of Sub-Committee no. 5;* supplements 1–3 (Washington: U. S. Government Printing Office, 1948) (80th Congress, 2d Session, House Document 619). Reprinted as *Communism, Its Plans and Tactics* (Washington: Infantry Journal Press, 1949), 102 pp.

DEMOCRACY VS COMMUNISM: THE STRUGGLE FOR MEN'S MINDS

Ascoli, Max, *The Power of Freedom* (New York: Farrar, Straus & Co., Inc., 1949), 173 pp.

Carroll, Wallace, *Persuade or Perish* (Boston: Houghton Mifflin Company, 1948), 392 pp.

"How Can We Win the War of Ideas?" [Radio Discussion by Paul Hoffman and Others] in *Town Meeting,* XVI, no. 51 (April 17, 1951), pp. 1–13.

LaFarge, John, *No Postponement; United States Moral Leadership and the Problem of Racial Minorities* (New York: Longmans Green and Company, 1950), 246 pp.

MacIver, Robert M., *The Ramparts We Guard* (New York: The Macmillan Company, 1950), 152 pp.

Schlesinger, Arthur M., Jr., *The Vital Center; The Politics of Freedom* (Boston: Houghton Mifflin Company, 1949), 274 pp.

"The Struggle for the Minds of Men," in Academy of Political Science, *Proceedings,* XXIV, no. 2 (January 1951), part II, pp. 212–262.

Thomson, Charles A. H., *Overseas Information Service of the United States Government* (Washington: Brookings Institution, 1949), 397 pp.

U. S. Congress, Senate, Committee on Foreign Relations, *Expanded International Information and Education Program; Hearings Before Subcommittee of Foreign Relations Committee on S.Res.243, 81st Congress, 2d Session, July 5–7, 1950* (Washington: U. S. Government Printing Office, 1950), 165 pp.

U. S. Department of State, *Telling America's Story Abroad* (Washington: U. S. Government Printing Office, 1951), 28 pp. (International Information and Cultural Series 14, Pub. 4079)

RESPONSIBILITIES OF BUSINESS LEADERSHIP

Abrams, Frank W., "Management's Responsibilities in a Complex World," in *Harvard Business Review,* XXIX, no. 3 (May 1951), pp. 29–34).

Allen, George Howard, ed., *Individual Initiative in Business* (Cambridge: Harvard University Press, 1950), 255 pp. Selected Bibliography: pp. 241–255. (Addresses given at the 20th Annual Conference of the Harvard Business School Alumni Association, June 10, 1950)

Barnard, Chester I., *Organization and Management; Selected Papers* (Cambridge: Harvard University Press, 1948), 244 pp.

Bower, Marvin, ed., *The Development of Executive Leadership* (Cambridge: Harvard University Press, 1949), 130 pp. (Addresses given at the 19th Annual Conference of the Harvard Business School Alumni Association, June 11, 1949)

David, Donald K., "Business Responsibilities in an Uncertain World," in *Harvard Business Review,* XXVII, no. 3, supplement (May 1949), 8 pp.

Dempsey, Bernard W., "The Roots of Business Responsibility," in *Harvard Business Review,* XXVII, no. 4 (July 1949), pp. 393–404.

Flanders, Ralph E., *The Function of Management in American Life;* lectures delivered at the Seventh Annual Business Conference, July 19–23, 1948 (Stanford: Stanford University Graduate School of Business, 1949), 52 pp.

Holman, Eugene, *The Public Responsibilities of Big Companies* (New York: Standard Oil Company of New Jersey, 1948), 11 pp. (An Address given at the Economic Club of Detroit, November 8, 1948)

Jones, Thomas Roy, "Obligations of Leadership in an Evolving Society," in *Dun's Review* (March 1949), pp. 11–13.

Merrill, Harwood F., ed., *The Responsibilities of Business Leadership* (Cambridge: Harvard University Press, 1948), 93 pp. (Addresses given at the 18th Annual Conference of the Harvard Business School Alumni Association, June 12, 1948.)

The Social Responsibilities of Management [Four lectures by] Stuart Chase, Stanley H. Ruttenberg, Edwin G. Nourse, William B. Given, Jr. (New York: School of Commerce, Accounts, and Finance, New York University, 1950), 83 pp. (The Edward L. Bernays Foundation Lectures of 1950)

Economic and Industrial Mobilization

Bureau of National Affairs, Inc., *Daily Report for Executives* (Washington) (A daily service covering important Washington developments affecting business, taxation and finance, and industrial and agricultural commodities)

Commerce Clearing House, *Emergency Business Control Law Reports* (Chicago) (A loose-leaf business service covering federal controls)

Committee for Economic Development, *Economic Policy for Rearmament* (New York, 1950), 22 pp.

"The Economic Impact of the Rearmament Program," Institute of International Finance, *The I.I.F. Bulletin,* no. 169 (December 12, 1950), 18 pp.

Harris, Seymour E., *The Economics of America at War* (New York: W. W. Norton & Company, Inc., 1943), 418 pp.

Harris, Seymour E., "Major Economic Problems of Mobilization," in *Harvard Business Review,* XXIX, no. 2 (March 1951), pp. 29–36.

Janeway, Eliot, "American Security: Lowest Common Denominator," in *Harvard Business Review,* XXIX, no. 4 (July 1951), pp. 115–124. (A second article by Mr. Janeway entitled "The Drive and Direction of Mobilization" appeared in the *Harvard Business Review,* September 1951)

Krout, John A., ed., *Mobilizing American Power for Defense* (New York: Academy of Political Science, 1951), 154 pp. (*Proceedings of the Academy of Political Science,* XXIV, no. 3)

Lincoln, George A., William S. Stone, and Thomas H. Harvey, eds., *Economics of National Security* (New York: Prentice-Hall, Inc., 1950), 601 pp. Bibliographies at end of most chapters.

McNair, Malcolm P., "This New Kind of War—What Does It Take to Win?" (Address given at the Great Lakes Business Conference, Cleveland, Ohio, April 7, 1951. Published in the *Harvard Business School Bulletin,* XXVII, no. 2, Summer 1951)

National Industrial Conference Board, *The Conference Board Economic Forum Presents: The Business Outlook, 1951* (New York, 1951), 52 pp. (Studies in Business Economics, No. 27)

National Industrial Conference Board, *Industrial Mobilization Planning* (New York, 1949), 36 pp. (Studies in Business Policy, No. 35)

National Industrial Conference Board, *Mobilizing for Atomic War* (New York, 1950), 64 pp. (Studies in Business Policy, No. 46)

Nelson, Donald M., *Arsenal of Democracy; the Story of American War Production* (New York: Harcourt Brace and Company, 1946), 439 pp.

"Problems of an Advanced Defense Economy," in *American Economic Review,* Papers and Proceedings, XL, no. 2 (May 1950), pp. 191–233.

"Proceedings on Economic Mobilization Short of War," Presented at the Annual Meeting of the American Economic Association, Chicago, December 29, 1950, in *American Economic Review,* XLI, no. 1 (March 1951), pp. 51–76.

Shaw, Edward S., and Lorie Tarshis, "A Program for Economic Mobilization," in *American Economic Review,* XLI, no. 1 (March 1951), pp. 30–50. ("Condensation of a larger study which will be published by the McGraw-Hill Book Co., Inc.")

Slichter, Sumner H., "Economic Problems of a Defense Economy," in *Commercial and Financial Chronicle,* CLXXII, no. 4952 (October 19, 1950), p. 1. (Address before the Fall Management Conference of the National Savings and Loan League, New York City, October 16, 1950)

Slichter, Sumner H., *What's Ahead for American Business* (Boston: Little, Brown and Company, 1951), 216 pp.

Smaller War Plants Corporation, *Economic Concentration and World War II; Report . . . to the Special Committee to Study Problems of American Small Business, United States Senate* (Washington: U. S. Government Printing Office, 1946), 359 pp.

"Thinking Ahead" [How to Achieve Sustained Readiness in the Present Crisis] by Edmund P. Learned, Malcolm P. McNair, et al., in *Harvard Business Review,* XXIX, no. 1 (January 1951), pp. 13–16.

"This Is the Year," in *Fortune,* XLIII, no. 1 (January 1951), pp. 53–60.

U. S. Congress, Senate, Committee on Banking and Currency, *Defense Production Act of 1950; Hearings . . . 81st Congress, 2d Session on S.3936 . . . July 24, 25 and 26, 1950* (Washington: U. S. Government Printing Office, 1950), 329 pp.

U. S. Council of Economic Advisers, *The Economics of National Defense; Fifth Annual Report to the President, December 1950* (Washington, 1950), 31 pp.

U. S. Library of Congress, Legislative Reference Service, *Mobilization Planning and National Security (1950–1960), Problems and Issues* (Washington: U. S. Government Printing Office, 1950), 245 pp. (81st Congress, 2d Session, Document no. 204)

U. S. National Production Authority, *Defense Production Record* (Weekly). I, no. 1 (May 3, 1951–to date).

U. S. Office of Defense Mobilization, *Quarterly Report to the President* (Washington: U. S. Government Printing Office), no. 1, April 1, 1951, "Building America's Might"; no. 2, July 1, 1951, "Meeting Defense Goals a *Must* for Everyone."

U. S. President, *The Economic Report of the President Transmitted to the Congress . . . Together with a Report to the President, The Annual Eco-*

nomic Review by the Council of Economic Advisers (Washington: U. S. Government Printing Office) (Latest annual report, January 12, 1951; Midyear report, July 1951)

"We'll Be Mighty within 3 Years; an Interview with Charles E. Wilson," in *U. S. News & World Report,* XXX, no. 12 (March 23, 1951), pp. 30–35.

"What the War Taught Us about Materials Control, Price Control, Wage Control, Military Procurement," in *Dun's Review,* January 1951. (Four separate articles by authorities in the specialized fields)

FISCAL POLICY AND INFLATION

Abbott, Charles C., "Thinking Ahead" [Prospective Costs of Mobilization and Their Effect on the Economy] in *Harvard Business Review,* XXIX, no. 3 (May 1951), pp. 17–18.

Committee for Economic Development, *Paying for Defense; A Statement on National Policy* (New York, 1950), 48 pp.

Committee on Federal Tax Policy, *Financing Defense; Can Expenditure Be Reduced?* (New York, 1951), 31 pp.

Federal Reserve Bank of Philadelphia, *Problems in a Mobilized Economy* (36th Annual Report, 1950) (Philadelphia, 1951), pp. 1–32.

Hart, Albert G., *Defense without Inflation* (New York: Twentieth Century Fund, 1951), 186 pp. (The first of a projected series of at least four volumes)

Hart, Albert G., et al., *Financing Defense; Federal Tax and Expenditure Policies* (New York: Twentieth Century Fund, 1951), 161 pp. (The second in a series. To be followed by reports on the use of direct controls, and on monetary and fiscal policies)

U. S. Congress, Joint Committee on the Economic Report, *Economic and Political Hazards of an Inflationary Defense Economy* (Washington: U. S. Government Printing Office, 1951), 96 pp. (82d Congress, 1st Session, Joint Committee Print)

U. S. Congress, Joint Committee on the Economic Report, *General Credit Control, Debt Management, and Economic Mobilization* (Washington: U. S. Government Printing Office, 1951), 98 pp. (82d Congress, 1st Session, Joint Committee Print)

COMPANY DEFENSE PLANS

American Management Association, *Financial Planning for Defense Production,* with three papers on Borrowing from Banks and Insurance Companies (New York, 1951), 48 pp. (Financial Management Series, No. 98)

National Industrial Conference Board, *Decentralization in Industry* (New York, 1948), 40 pp. (Studies in Business Policy, No. 30)

National Industrial Conference Board, *Industrial Standardization; Company Organization Practices and Procedures* (New York, 1947), 64 pp. (Studies in Business Policy, No. 22)

National Industrial Conference Board, *Military Inspection in Industry* (New York, 1951), 76 pp. (Studies in Business Policy, No. 50)

National Industrial Conference Board, *Protecting Records in Wartime* (New York, 1951), 40 pp. (Studies in Business Policy, No. 51)

"Report on Rearmament," in *Fortune,* XLIII, no. 4 (April 1951), pp. 93–98.
Research Institute of America, Inc., *Adjusting to Mobilization, 1950* (New York, 1950), 48 pp. (Analysis 74)
Tupper, Ernest A., "Guidepost to Industrial Mobilization [Background, Considerations and Problems of Business Policy-Making in a Semi-Mobilized Economy]," in *Harvard Business Review,* XXVIII, no. 6 (November 1950), pp. 29–44.
"War Mobilization Check List," Special Issue of *Management Guide,* 1950, pp. 19,000–19,021.

MANPOWER AND INDUSTRIAL RELATIONS

Allen, Louis A., "Mobilization on the Production Front," in *Mill and Factory,* XLVIII, no. 3 (March 1951), pp. 89–92.
American Management Association, *Personnel Problems under Mobilization,* with a section on Economic and Political Factors (New York, 1950), 62 pp. (Personnel Series, No. 135)
Bureau of National Affairs, Inc., *Military Leave Policies of 500 Corporations* (Washington, 1950), 28 pp.
Goodwin, Robert C., "Prepare for Tomorrow's Manpower Problems," in *Mill and Factory,* XLVIII, no. 1 (January 1951), pp. 75–79.
Industrial Relations Counselors, Inc., *Impact of Mobilization on Industrial Relations* (New York, 1950), 24 pp. (Industrial Relations Memos, No. 118)
"Manpower Controls Next?" in *Fortune,* XLIII, no. 3 (March 1951), pp. 78–79.
"Manpower Potential for National Security." Special Issue of the U. S. Bureau of Employment Security, *The Labor Market and Employment Security* (August 25, 1950), 44 pp.
Metropolitan Life Insurance Company, Policyholders Service Bureau, *Manpower Planning for National Emergency* (New York, 1950), 68 pp.
"Training Manpower," in *Fortune,* XLIII, no. 4 (April 1951), pp. 116–119.

PRICE AND WAGE CONTROLS

American Management Association, *Wage Policy and Problems in a Preparedness Economy* (New York, 1950), 35 pp. (Personnel Series, No. 136)
"Arms and the Price System," in *Fortune,* XLII, no. 6 (December 1950), pp. 80–83.
Committee for Economic Development, *Conditions Necessary for Effective Wage-Price Control* (New York, 1951), 8 pp.
Field, Richard H., "Economic Stabilization under the Defense Production Act of 1950," in *Harvard Law Review,* LXIV, no. 1 (November 1950), pp. 1–26.
Galbraith, J. Kenneth, "The Strategy of Limited Control," in *Fortune,* XLIII, no. 3 (March 1951), pp. 66–67.
National Industrial Conference Board, *The Conference Board Economic Forum Presents: Price Control in a Defense Economy* (New York, 1950), 64 pp. (Studies in Business Economics, No. 26)
National Industrial Conference Board, *Wage Stabilization; Orders—Regulations—Interpretation* (New York, 1951). (A loose-leaf supplement to the Conference Board Management Record.)

Research Institute of America, Inc., *Research Institute Guide to Price Control* (New York, 1951), 48 pp. (Analysis 82)

Reuther, Walter P., *Wage Stabilization and Defense Mobilization; A Transcript of Testimony before the Wage Stabilization Board* (Washington, 1950), 37 pp.

U. S. Bureau of Labor Statistics, *Problems and Policies of Dispute Settlement and Wage Stabilization During World War II* (Washington, 1950), 380 pp. (Bulletin No. 1009)

U. S. Office of Temporary Controls, *Studies in Industrial Price Control* [in Iron and Steel Industry] (Washington: U. S. Government Printing Office, 1946), 181 pp. (Historical Report on War Administration: Office of Price Administration, General Publication No. 6)

PROCUREMENT AND MATERIALS CONTROL

Ashler, Philip F., "Small Business and Defense Contracts," in *Harvard Business Review*, XXIX, no. 3 (May 1951), pp. 104–112.

Bureau of National Affairs, Inc., *CMP Takes Over; a Special Report* (Washington, 1951), 66 pp.

Bureau of National Affairs, Inc., *Selling to the Federal Government; A Comprehensive Guidebook* (Washington, 1949), 348 pp.

"How to Get a CMP Allotment and Operate Under the Program's Rules," in *Factory Management and Maintenance*, CIX, no. 5 (May 1951), pp. W1–W16 inserted between pp. 64–65.

"Industry Suggests: Cures for Material Shortages (Survey of Business Opinion)," in National Industrial Conference Board, *The Conference Board Business Record*, VIII, no. 3 (March 1951), pp. 96–101.

National Industrial Conference Board, *The Conference Board Presents: Key Materials; Current Supply and Outlook* (New York, 1951), 47 pp. (Studies in Business Economics, No. 28)

National Industrial Conference Board, *Renegotiation in Peace and War* (New York, 1950), 48 pp. (Studies in Business Policy, No. 44)

Novick, David, Melvin Anshen, and W. C. Truppner, *Wartime Production Controls* (New York: Columbia University Press, 1949), 441 pp.

U. S. Congress, House, Committee on Armed Services, *Stockpiling of Strategic and Critical Materials; Hearings before the Special Subcommittee of the Committee on Armed Services, House of Representatives, 81st Congress, 2d Session* (Washington: U. S. Government Printing Office, 1950), pp. 7471–7691.

U. S. Congress, Senate, Committee on Finance, *Renegotiation of Contracts; Hearings, 1st Session on H.R. 1724 . . . January 31 and February 2, 1951* (Washington: U. S. Government Printing Office, 1951), 139 pp.

U. S. Congress, Senate, Special Committee to Study Problems of American Small Business, *Participation of Small Business in Government Procurement; A Final Report . . . 80th Congress, 2d Session, Pursuant to S.Res. 20* (Washington: U. S. Government Printing Office, 1949), 22 pp. (81st Congress, 1st Session, Senate, Report No. 45)

U. S. Defense Production Administration, *Mobilization Guide for Small Business* (Washington, 1951), 31 pp.

U. S. Munitions Board, *Military Procurement; A Guide for Joint Industry-Military Procurement Planning* (Washington: U. S. Government Printing Office, 1948), 46 pp.

U. S. Munitions Board, *Production Allocation Manual; Production Planning for Emergency Procurement* (Washington: U. S. Government Printing Office, 1950), 83 pp.

U. S. Munitions Board, *Stockpile Report to the Congress, January 23, 1951* (Washington, 1951), 39 pp. (A semi-annual report)

"What CMP Will Be Like [An Interview with Manly Fleischmann]," in *Business Week*, no. 1129 (April 21, 1951), p. 136.

Worsley, Thomas B., *Wartime Economic Stabilization and the Efficiency of Government Procurement; A Critical Analysis of Certain Experience of the United States in World War II* (Washington: U. S. Government Printing Office, 1949), 422 pp. Bibliography, pp. 397–422.

ECONOMIC AND ARMED MOBILIZATION OF OUR ALLIES

Bissell, Richard M., Jr., "The Impact of Rearmament on the Free World Economy," in *Foreign Affairs*, XXIX, no. 3 (April 1951), pp. 385–405.

Bloch, Ernest, "European Rearmament and United States Foreign Aid," in *Review of Economics and Statistics*, XXXII, no. 4 (November 1950), pp. 339–346.

Daniels, Walter M., comp., *Defense of Western Europe* (New York: H. W. Wilson Company, 1950), 242 pp. (Reference Shelf, v.XXII, No. 5) Bibliography, pp. 218–242.

Dean, Vera Micheles, and Howard C. Gray, *Military and Economic Strength of Western Europe* (New York: Foreign Policy Association, 1950), pp. 118–128. (*Foreign Policy Reports*, XXVI, no. 11, October 15, 1950)

"The Defense of Europe," in *Fortune*, XLII no. 4 (October 1950), pp. 76–79.

Gavin, Leon Harry, "Status of Our Defense in Europe," in *Commercial and Financial Chronicle*, CLXXIII, no. 4982 (February 1, 1951), p. 11; No. 4984 (February 8, 1951), p. 23.

Head, A. H., "European Defence," in *International Affairs*, XXVII, no. 1 (January 1951), pp. 1–9.

Kennedy, John F., "Issues in the Defense of Europe," in *Commercial and Financial Chronicle*, CLXXIII, no. 4986 (February 15, 1951), p. 21.

Krout, John A., ed., *The Defense of the Free World* (New York: Academy of Political Science, 1951), 138 pp. (*Proceedings of the Academy of Political Science*, XXIV, no. 2)

McLachlan, Donald H., "Rearmament and European Integration," in *Foreign Affairs*, XXIX, no. 2 (January 1951), pp. 276–286.

Robinson, E. A. G., "The Economics of Rearmament," in *Lloyd's Bank Review*, new series, no. 19 (January 1951), pp. 15–32.

Royal Institute of International Affairs, *Defense in the Cold War; The Task for the Free World* (London, 1950), 123 pp.

Bei Fragen zur Produktsicherheit wenden Sie sich bitte an:
If you have any questions regarding product safety,
please contact:

Walter de Gruyter GmbH
Genthiner Straße 13
10785 Berlin
productsafety@degruyterbrill.com